4

JUNIOR

CLASSICS

Published in Red Turtle by
Rupa Publications India Pvt. Ltd 2016
7/16, Ansari Road, Daryaganj
New Delhi 110002

Sales centres:
Allahabad Bengaluru Chennai
Hyderabad Jaipur Kathmandu
Kolkata Mumbai

ISBN: 978-81-291-3888-0

First impression 2016

10 9 8 7 6 5 4 3 2 1

Printed in India by Replika Press Pvt. Ltd.

Contents

Heidi
Johanna Spyri

Two figures were walking along a green mountain path on a June morning. One, a tall strong-looking girl, the other, a child. Though it was summer, the child was dressed in layers of clothes. They were making their way to the hamlet known as Dorfli, which was half-way up the mountain. The elder girl greeted the people that she met on the way. Her name was Deta.

She was taking the younger girl, Heidi, to her grandfather's house, up the mountain. His hut stood on a rock, exposed to the winds. Behind the hut stood three old fir trees, with long thick branches.

The old man was sitting outside the hut, his pipe in his mouth. Heidi was at the top first. She went straight up to the old man, put out her hand, and said, 'Good evening, Grandfather.'

'Well, well, what does that mean?' he asked gruffly.

Deta, who was Heidi's aunt, had arrived in the meantime with Peter, the goatherd, who lived on the mountain in a hut with his mother and grandmother. Peter was eager to see what was happening.

'I wish you good-day, Uncle,' said Deta, as she walked towards him, 'and I have brought you Tobias and Adelheid's child. The child is here to remain with you.'

'Uncle, I have brought the little girl for you to keep,' said Deta. 'I have done my share these last four years and now it is your turn to provide for her.'

The old man rose from his seat. He looked at Deta in a way that made her draw back a step or two, then flinging out his arm, he said to her in a commanding voice, 'Be off with you this instant, and get back as quickly as you can to the place whence you came, and do not let me see your face again in a hurry.'

Deta did not wait to be told twice.

'Goodbye to you then, and to you too, Heidi,' she called, as she turned quickly away and started to come down the mountain at a running pace.

As soon as Deta left, the old man went back to his bench. Heidi, meanwhile, explored everything outside the hut.

'I want to see what you have inside the house,' said Heidi.

'Come then!' and the grandfather rose and went before her towards the hut.

'Take your things along,' he said.

'I do not want them anymore,' said Heidi.

The old man, turning about, threw a glance at her. The child's black eyes were sparkling in expectation of all the things to come.

'She is not lacking in intelligence,' he whispered to himself. Aloud he added, 'Why don't you need them anymore?'

'I want to go about like the light-footed goats!'

'All right, you can; but bring the things and we'll put them in the cupboard.'

Heidi did as she was told. She found herself in a good-sized room, which covered the whole ground floor of the hut.

'Where am I to sleep, grandfather?'

'Wherever you like,' he said.

Heidi was awakened early the next morning by Peter's loud whistle.

'Do you want to go with Peter and the goats on to the mountain?' asked her grandfather. Nothing could have pleased Heidi more, and she jumped for joy in answer.

One day, Heidi went running hither and thither and shouting with delight, for here were whole patches of delicate red primroses, and there the blue gleam of the lovely gentian, while above them all laughed and nodded the tender-leaved golden cistus. Happy with all this waving field of brightly coloured flowers, Heidi forgot even Peter and the goats. All the while she was plucking handfuls of the flowers which she put into her little apron, for she wanted to take them all home and stick them in the hay, so that she might make her bedroom look just like the meadows.

'Where have you got to now, Heidi?' Peter said, somewhat harshly.

'Here,' called back a voice from somewhere. She sat surrounded by the flowers, drawing in deep breaths of the scented air.

'It is time for dinner,' he said.

Heidi sat down.

'Is the milk for me?' she asked, looking at the beautifully arranged square with the bowl as a chief ornament in the centre.

'Yes,' said Peter, 'and the two large pieces of bread and cheese are yours also, and when you have drunk up that milk, you are to have another bowlful from the white goat, and then it will be my turn.'

'And where do you get your milk from?' inquired Heidi.

'From my own goat. But go on now with your dinner,' said Peter.

Heidi now took up the bowl and drank her milk, and as soon as she had put it down empty Peter rose and filled it again for her. Then she broke off a piece of her bread and held out the remainder, which was still larger than Peter's own piece, together with the whole big slice of cheese, saying, 'You can have that, I have plenty.'

Peter looked at Heidi, shocked for a moment, for never in all his life could he have said and done like that with anything he had. He seized the food, thanked her and then made the most splendid meal that he had known ever since he became a goatherd. Heidi continued to watch the goats.

She grew strong and healthy. She was happy too, and lived from day to day as free and lighthearted as a little bird. Then the autumn came, and the wind blew louder and stronger. Heidi met Peter's blind grandmother and grew to love her. After many years of joyless life, the blind grandmother had at last found something to make her happy. She listened for the little tripping footsteps first thing every day, and when she heard the door open and knew the child was really there, she would call out, 'God be thanked, she has come again!' And Heidi would sit by her and talk in so lively a manner that the grandmother never noticed how the time went by.

Heidi had been in the mountains for three years now and was eight years old. She had learnt all kinds of useful things from her grandfather; she knew how to look after their two goats—the white Little Swan and the brown Little Bear that would follow her like two faithful dogs, and give a loud bleat of pleasure when they heard her voice.

One day, before the dinner bowls had been cleared away, a visitor arrived, and this time it was cousin Deta. She had a fine feathered hat on her head, and a long trailing skirt to her dress which swept the floor.

Deta had prepared a speech and started with saying how well Heidi looked and that it was evident that she had been happy and well-cared for with her grandfather; but she had never lost sight of the idea of taking the child back again. A wealthy family in Frankfurt wanted a child companion for their only daughter who was ill and bedridden. They wanted a simple-minded and unspoilt child, and not like most of the children that one saw nowadays. Deta had thought at once of Heidi.

'You may take your niece to anybody you like, I will have nothing to do with it,' said the grandfather.

But Deta shouted, 'She is my own sister's child. I am responsible for what happens to her!'

'Be silent!'

'You have made grandfather angry,' said Heidi.

'He will soon be all right again; come now,' said Deta hurriedly, 'and show me where your clothes are.'

'I am not coming,' said Heidi.

'Nonsense,' said Deta. Then she went to the cupboard and taking out Heidi's things, she rolled them up in a bundle. 'Come along now.' Deta had now got the bundle under her arm and the child by the hand, and so they went down the mountain together.

In her home in Frankfurt, Clara, the little daughter of Herr Sesemann, was lying on the invalid couch on which she spent her days, being wheeled in it from room to room. Clara's little face was thin and pale, and at this moment her two soft blue eyes were fixed on the clock.

'Isn't it time yet, Fraulein Rottenmeier?'

This lady was sitting erect at a small work-table, busy with her embroidery. She had on a mysterious-looking loose garment, a large collar or shoulder-cape that gave a certain solemnity to her appearance, which was enhanced by a very lofty dome-shaped head dress. For many years past, since the mistress of the house had died, the housekeeping had been handed over by Herr Sesemann to Fraulein Rottenmeier. He himself was often away from home, and left her in sole charge.

Deta and Heidi arrived at the front door and went upstairs into the study. Fraulein Rottenmeier rose slowly and went up to the little new companion for the daughter of the house, to see what she was like. She did not seem very pleased with her appearance. Heidi was dressed in her plain little woollen frock, and her hat was an old straw one bent out of shape.

'What is your name?' asked Fraulein Rottenmeier.

'Heidi,' she said in a clear, loud voice.

'What is your real name?' continued Fraulein Rottenmeier.

'I do not remember,' replied Heidi.

'She was named after her mother, my sister, Adelheid, who is now dead,' said Deta.

'Well, that's a name that one can pronounce,' said Fraulein Rottenmeier. 'But I must tell you, Deta, that I am astonished to see so young a child. I told you that I wanted a companion of the same age as the young lady of the house, one who could share her lessons, and all her other occupations. Fraulein Clara is now over twelve; what age is this child?'

'Grandfather told me I was eight,' put in Heidi.

'What, only eight!' said Fraulein Rottenmeier angrily. 'Four years too young! Of what use is such a child! And what have you learnt? What books did you have to learn from?'

'None,' said Heidi. 'I have never learnt to read, or Peter either,' she added.

'Mercy upon us! You do not know how to read! Is it really so?' said Fraulein Rottenmeier, greatly shocked.

Heidi remained by the door where she had been standing since she first came in. Clara had looked on during the interview without speaking; now she beckoned to Heidi and said, 'Come here!' Heidi went up to her.

'Would you rather be called Heidi or Adelheid?' asked Clara.

'I am never called anything but Heidi,' was the child's prompt answer.

'Are you pleased to come to Frankfurt?' said Clara.

'No, but I shall go home soon,' said Heidi.

'Well, you are a funny child!' said Clara.

Heidi lived in the Sesemann's house for a year. The best part of her stay was that Clara taught her how to read. But for most of the time, she was bored or getting into trouble.

One evening, at dinner Heidi's eyes lit up when she saw a white bread roll on her plate. She wanted to save it for Peter's grandmother in case she ever saw her again.

'Can I have it?' she asked Sebastian, the kind butler.

He nodded, throwing a side glance at Fraulein Rottenmeier to see what effect this request would have upon her. Heidi immediately grabbed the roll and put it in her pocket. Sebastian's face became twisted because he was overcome with laughter but knew his place too well to laugh out loud. Mute and motionless, he still remained standing beside Heidi; it was not his duty to speak, nor to move away until she had helped herself.

Heidi had already made a decision to go back where she came from. On her way out, she encountered Fraulein Rottenmeier who stared at Heidi in surprise.

'What are you upto? Haven't I forbidden you to run away? You look like a vagabond!'

'I was only going home,' whispered the frightened child.

'What, you want to run away from this house? What would Herr Sesemann say? What is it that does not suit you here? Don't you get better treatment than you deserve? Have you ever before had such food, service and such a room? Answer!'

'No,' was the reply.

'Don't I know that?' said Fraulein Rottenmeier. 'What a thankless child you are, just idle and good-for-nothing!'

Heidi began to cry every so often because she missed the mountains and her grandfather.

A few days after her attempt to escape, Herr Sesemann returned home. Heidi was sitting beside Clara when he came to see them. Father and daughter greeted each other with warm affection, for they were deeply attached to one another. Then he held out his hand to Heidi and said kindly to her, 'And this is our little Swiss girl; come and shake hands with me! That's right! Now, tell me, are Clara and you good friends with one another?

'Clara is always kind to me,' said Heidi.

'And Heidi,' put in Clara quickly, 'has not once tried to quarrel.'

'That's all right, I am glad to hear it,' said her father.

Herr Sesemann was only home for a short time; he left for Paris again before the fortnight was over, comforting Clara by telling her that her grandmother would soon come visiting.

The day arrived before they knew it. As Heidi opened the study door, she heard a kind voice say, 'Ah, here comes the child! Come along in and let me have a good look at you.'

Heidi walked up to her and said very distinctly in her clear voice, 'Good evening, Mrs Madam.'

'Well!' said the grandmother, laughing, 'Is that how they address people in your home on the mountain?'

'No,' said Heidi gravely, 'I never knew anyone with that name before.'

'Nor I either,' said the grandmother again as she patted Heidi's cheek. 'Never mind! When I am with the children I am always grandmamma; you won't forget that name, will you?'

'No, no,' said Heidi. 'I often used to say it at home.'

'I understand,' said the grandmother, with a cheerful little nod of the head. She had such beautiful white hair, and two long lace ends hung down from the cap on her head and waved gently about her face every time she moved.

'And what is your name, child?' the grandmother now asked.

'I am always called Heidi but as I am now to be called Adelheid, I will try and take care—' Heidi stopped short, for she was not yet used to this name.

'Frau Sesemann will no doubt agree with me,' said Frau Rottenmeier, 'that it was necessary to choose a name that could be pronounced easily, if only for the sake of the servants.'

'My worthy Rottenmeier,' said Frau Sesemann, 'if a person is called 'Heidi' and has grown accustomed to that name, I call her by the same, and so let it be.'

Heidi and Clara's grandmother had an instant affection for each other that annoyed Fraulein Rottenmeier.

One night Clara's grandmother showed Heidi a storybook with pictures of pastures and trees. This made Heidi cry and she told the grandmother about her life in the mountains, about the goats, Peter, her grandfather, and Peter's grandmother.

Each day after that, Heidi grew sadder and sadder. Her eyes no longer held the bright spark that they once did.

The day came for grandmother's departure, a sad one for Clara and Heidi. But the grandmother was determined to make it as much like a holiday as possible and not to let them mope, and she kept them so lively and amused that they had no time to think about their sorrow at her going until she really drove away.

And so many weeks passed away. Heidi did not know if it was winter or summer, for the walls and windows she looked out upon showed no change, and she never went beyond the house except on rare occasions when Clara was well enough to drive out, and then they only went a very little way, as Clara could not bear the movement for long.

Heidi began to sleepwalk and the rest of the house thought it was a ghost that left all the doors open at night. But one day, Herr Sesemann discovered that it was her when he sat on watch for the ghost.

He called for a doctor to check Heidi. 'Sesemann,' the doctor said, 'the child is consumed with homesickness, to such an extent that she is nearly a skeleton already, and soon will be quite one; something must be done at once. There is but one remedy, to send her back to her native mountain air.'

Herr Sesemann made immediate arrangements to send Heidi home. He sent for Sebastian, the butler, and told him to travel with the child as far as Basle that day, and the next day take her home. Heidi was fetched, and she walked up to Herr Sesemann to say 'Good morning.'

'Why, you don't know anything about it, I see,' said Herr Sesemann. 'You are going home today, going at once.'

'Home,' said Heidi in a low voice. She could hardly breathe.

'Come along, Heidi,' said Clara, as she entered 'see all the things I have had put in for you. Aren't you pleased?'

In their delight the children forgot that the time had come for them to separate, and when someone called out, 'The carriage is here,' there was no time for complaining.

Just outside the station, Sebastian saw a shabby-looking little cart and horse which a broad-shouldered man was loading with heavy sacks. He went up to him and asked if he would take Heidi to Dorfli.

'I can go by myself, I know the way well from Dorfli,' put in Heidi.

Sebastian lifted Heidi and her basket on to the high seat and shook hands with her. The cart rolled away in the direction of the mountains.

The man dropped her off at the village. Heidi climbed up the steep path from Dorfli as quickly as she could. One thought alone filled Heidi's mind, 'Would she find the grandmother sitting in her usual corner by the spinning-wheel, was she still alive?' She ran faster and faster and her heart beat louder and louder. She had reached the house.

'Ah, my God!' said a voice from the corner, 'that was how Heidi used to run in; if only I could have her with me once again! Who is there?'

'It's I, grandmother,' said Heidi as she ran and flung herself on her knees beside the old woman. And Heidi took the rolls from the basket and put them all on the grandmother's lap.

'Ah, child! Child! What a blessing you bring with you!' the old woman exclaimed.

'I must go home to grandfather,' she said, 'but tomorrow I shall come again. Goodnight, grandmother.'

Heidi continued her way up the mountain. All around her the steep green slopes shone bright in the evening sun, and soon the great shining snow-field up above came in sight. Then there was grandfather sitting as in old days smoking his pipe, and she could see the fir trees waving in the wind. Quicker and quicker went her little feet, and before Grandfather had time to see who was coming, Heidi had rushed up to him, thrown down her basket and flung her arms round his neck.

The old man himself said nothing. For the first time for many years his eyes were wet, and he had to pass his hand across them.

'So you have come back to me, Heidi,' he said, 'Did they send you away?'

'Oh, no, grandfather,' said Heidi eagerly, 'You must not think that; they were all so kind. Clara, and grandmamma, and Herr Sesemann. But you see, grandfather, I was sick till I got home again to you.'

A shrill whistle was heard outside. Heidi rushed out like a flash of lightning. There were the goats leaping and jumping among the rocks, with Peter in their midst. When he caught sight of Heidi he stood still with astonishment and looked speechlessly at her. Heidi called out, 'Good evening, Peter,' and then ran in among the goats. 'Little Swan! Little Bear! Do you know me again?'

The first day Heidi and her grandfather went to church, everybody soon knew of Grandfather's presence, and kept on turning round to look at him. When the service was over Grandfather took Heidi by the hand, and made his way towards the pastor's house; the rest of the crowd looked curiously after him, some even following to see whether he went inside the pastor's house, which he did. Then they collected in groups, keeping their eyes on the pastor's door, watching to see whether Grandfather came out looking angry and quarrelsome.

Some adopted a new tone and expressed their opinion that Grandfather was not so bad after all as they thought. Others responded that they had always thought people had exaggerated about him, that if he was so bad he would be afraid to go inside the pastor's house. And so everybody began to feel quite friendly towards Grandfather.

Times passed by slowly. Heidi now went to school in Dorfli every morning and afternoon, and eagerly set to work to learn all that was taught there. She tried to make Peter come with her, but he refused. She then began to teach him to read herself.

One morning Peter came up to the hut with a delivery. Heidi read the address carefully then she ran back to the shed holding out her letter to her grandfather in high glee.

'From Frankfurt! From Clara! Would you like to hear it?'

'Dearest Heidi—We are coming to see you. Everything is packed and we shall start now in two or three days. Papa is not coming with us as he has first to go to Paris. Oh, how I am

looking forward to seeing everything and to being with you on the mountain, and to making the friendship of Peter and the goats. Your affectionate friend, Clara.'

May passed, everything started growing greener and greener, and then came the month of June, with a hotter sun and long light days. One day Heidi, having finished her domestic duties, ran out to play. But just as she was turning the corner of the hut, she gave such a loud cry that her grandfather came running out of the shed to see what had happened.

'Grandfather, grandfather!' she said, beside herself with excitement. 'Come here! Look! Look!'

The old man was by her side by this time and looked in the direction of her outstretched hand.

A strange looking march was making its way up the mountain; in front were two men carrying a sedan chair, in which sat a girl well wrapped up in shawls; then followed a horse, mounted by an elegant lady;

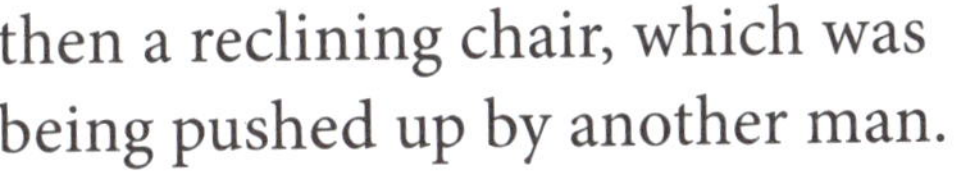

then a reclining chair, which was being pushed up by another man.

Clara was gazing around in a trance; she had never imagined, much less seen, anything so beautiful. Heidi wheeled Clara around in her chair, showing her everything she could.

'Oh, the flowers!' said Clara. 'Look at the bushes of red flowers, and all the nodding blue bells! Oh, if I could but get up and pick some!'

Heidi ran off at once and picked some flowers and made a large nosegay for Clara.

'But these are nothing, Clara,' she said, laying the flowers on her lap. 'If you could come up higher to where the goats are feeding, then you would indeed see something! Oh, it is beautiful up there, and if you sit down among them you never want to get up again, everything looks and smells so lovely!'

Peter came down with his goats. As soon as the animals caught sight of Heidi they all came flocking towards her, and she, as well as Clara on her couch, were soon surrounded by the goats, pushing and poking their heads one over the other, while Heidi introduced each in turn by its name to her friend.

Three weeks passed. Clara and Heidi would write letters, take walks in the mountains or sit under the fir trees and talk. Clara, who had never had an appetite for food, was always hungry for the milk, cheese and bread that Grandfather prepared.

One sunny day, they all decided to make their way to the valley of flowers. When they stopped on the way for a break, the wind blew Clara's wheelchair down a slope and it broke into pieces.

'It must have been the wind, Grandfather,' said Heidi. 'Oh! If it has blown the chair all the way down to Dorfli we shall not get it back in time, and shall not be able to go.'

'If it has rolled as far as that it will never come back, for it is in a hundred pieces by now,' said the grandfather, going round the corner and looking down.

'Oh, I am sorry,' said Clara, 'for we shall not be able to go today, or perhaps any other day. I shall have to go home, I suppose, if I have no chair. Oh, I am so sorry, I am so sorry!'

But Heidi looked towards her grandfather with her usual expression of confidence.

'Grandfather, you will be able to do something, won't you, so that it need not be as Clara says, and so that she is not obliged to go home?'

'Well, for the present we will go up the mountain as we had arranged, and then later on we will see what can be done,' he answered, much to the children's delight.

Grandfather carried Clara to the flower valley, then set her on her ground. He would come later and carry her home.

Clara watched Heidi and Peter playing among the flowers and expressed her wish to learn to walk. So Heidi and Peter held her and instructed her.

'Put your foot down firmly once,' said Heidi. Clara went on putting one foot out after another until all at once she called out, 'I can do it, Heidi! Look! Look! I can make proper steps!' And Heidi cried out with even greater delight, 'Can you really make steps, can you really walk? Really walk by yourself? Oh, if only grandfather

were here!' and she continued gleefully to say, 'You can walk now, Clara, you can walk!'

Clara still held on firmly to her supports, but with every step she felt safer on her feet, as all three became aware, and Heidi was beside herself with joy.

'Now we shall be able to come up here together every day, and go just where we like; and you will be able all your life to walk about as I do.'

They did not have to go far to reach the field of flowers, and could already catch sight of the cistus flowers glowing gold in the sun. As they came to the bushes of the bluebell flowers, with sunny, inviting patches of warm ground between them, Clara said, 'Mightn't we sit down here for a while?'

After a few hours, Grandfather came up to bring them. Heidi rushed forward to meet him as soon as he appeared, as she wanted to be the first to tell him the good news about Clara. She was so excited that she could hardly get her words out.

The next morning Grandfather suggested that they should now write to Clara's grandmother and ask her if she would come and pay them a visit as they had something new to show her.

The following days were some of the most joyous that Clara had spent on the mountain. She awoke each morning with a happy voice within her crying, 'I am well now! I am well now! I shan't have to go about in a chair, I can walk by myself like other people.'

The day finally came for grandmamma's visit. Heidi jumped up from time to time, looking down the mountain road, to see if there was any sign of her approach.

At last she saw the march winding up the mountain just in the order she had expected. First there was the guide, then the white horse with grandmamma seated upon it, and last of all the porter with a heavy bundle on his back.

At last it reached the top, and grandmamma was there looking down on the children from her horse. She no sooner saw them, however, sitting side by side, than she began quickly getting down, as she cried out in a shocked tone of voice, 'Why is this? Why are you not lying in your chair, Clara? What are you all thinking about?'

But even before she had got close to them she threw up her hands in astonishment, exclaiming further, 'Is it really you, dear child? Why, your cheeks have grown quite round and rosy! I should hardly have known you again!' And she was running forward to hug her, when Heidi slipped down from the seat, and with Clara leaning on her shoulder, the two children began walking along quite coolly and naturally.

Clara was actually walking steadily and uprightly beside Heidi, and now the two children came towards her with smiling faces and rosy cheeks. Laughing and crying Grandmamma ran to them and embraced first Clara and then Heidi, and then Clara again, unable to speak for joy.

'My dear Uncle! My dear Uncle! How much we have to thank you for! It is all your doing! It is your caring and nursing.'

'And God's good sun and mountain air,' he interrupted her, smiling.

Meanwhile Herr Sesemann, who had finished his business in Paris, had also been preparing a surprise. Without saying a word to his mother he got into the train one sunny morning and travelled that day to Basle; the next morning he continued his journey, for a great longing had seized him to see his little daughter from whom he had been separated the whole summer.

Herr Sesemann was delighted to have come to the last steep bit of his journey, in another minute or two he would be with his little daughter, and he pleased himself with the thought of her surprise. But the company above had seen his approaching figure and recognized who it was, and they were preparing something he little expected as a surprise on their part.

As he stepped on to the space in front of the hut two figures came towards him. Herr Sesemann suddenly stopped, staring at the two children, and all at once tears started to fill his eyes.

'Don't you know me, Papa?' called Clara to him, her face beaming with happiness. 'Am I looking so different from the last time you saw me?' Then Herr Sesemann ran to his child and clasped her in his arms.

The Sesemann family were so grateful to Heidi and Grandfather that they told them to ask for anything they wanted. Grandfather asked Herr Sesemann to look after Heidi when he died. Heidi asked for her bed in Frankfurt to be given to Peter's grandmother.

The Sesemann family stayed a while at Dorfli and then went back home to Frankfurt, but only on the promise that Heidi would visit them frequently. Heidi, her grandfather and Peter watched them go, each group as happy as the other.

A TALE
OF
TWO
CITIES
Charles Dickens

It was the best of times,
it was the worst of times,
it was the age of wisdom,
it was the age of foolishness,
it was the epoch of belief,
it was the epoch of incredulity,
it was the season of Light,
it was the season of Darkness,
it was the spring of hope,
it was the winter of despair

It was England and France in 1775; and we had everything before us, we had nothing before us, we were all going direct to heaven and we were all going direct the other way. The conflict was clear as the gap between the ruler and the ruled increased manifold. Crimes were at an all-time high and other social ills bothered the two countries.

It was a Friday night in November. A mail coach was negotiating its way, via Shooter's Hill, from London to Dover in the darkness. The guard suspected the three passengers, the passengers suspected one another and the guard, they all suspected everybody else, and the coachman was sure of nothing but the horses.

It was no surprise that they were terrified when they heard a horse galloping towards their carriage. Soon, the follower almost overtook them.

'Is that the Dover mail?' the horseman demanded.

'Why do you want to know?' replied the guard.

'I want a passenger, if it is.'

'What passenger?'

'Mr Jarvis Lorry.'

One of the passengers had recognized the man, 'Who wants me? Is it Jerry?'

Jerry Cruncher was a messenger from Tellson's Bank and Jarvis Lorry, a clerk at the bank, received a short note that read, 'Wait at Dover for Mam'selle.' Jerry left immediately.

Every human creature is a deep secret and mystery to every other. The three passengers were a living example, with their unspoken negative impressions about each other. In the meantime, the mail coach lumbered, jolted, rattled and bumped upon its tedious way.

Between naps, sixty-year-old Lorry saw dreams about the bank and his mission, which was to dig someone out of a grave who was buried alive eighteen years ago. The other two passengers were also dozing.

The coach reached Dover in the morning and Mr Lorry checked into the Royal George Hotel. He dressed formally, had a quick breakfast and met Lucie Manette, who had arrived a while ago at the hotel. Lucie was the lady, who was referred to as the Mam'selle in the note the previous night.

The lady was informed that Mr Lorry would accompany her to France. When she learnt that her father, Doctor Alexandre Manette, was alive and living in France, she fainted. All along she had been living as an orphan, whose financial powers were under the care of Mr Lorry's bank.

On the other side of the ocean, on a street in Saint Antoine—a suburb in Paris—people had gathered after a large cask of wine had been dropped and broken. They were squeezing and pressing to extract the wine as much as much as possible. Someone from the crowd dipped his finger in the spilled liquid and wrote in bold on the wall—BLOOD.

The wine shopkeeper, thirty-year-old Monsieur Defarge was watching the event with his wife. Then, a moment later, the wife gestured that they had visitors. The shopkeeper had been talking to three men, who were all named Jacques.

The visitors, he found, were Mr Jarvis Lorry and Miss Manette. When the bank clerk introduced himself, they were taken to the fifth floor of the filthy apartment with the wine shop on the ground floor.

When they entered the room, they saw the man they had come to meet. He was a Frenchman who was also a former doctor. He was occupied in stitching shoes. He was aged and looked unfit. He was Lucie's father, Alexandre Manette, who had been a prisoner for eighteen years. His confused state was apparent when he was asked his name.

'One Hundred and Five, North Tower,' he said and repeated, 'One Hundred and Five, North Tower.'

Then, he bent and returned to his work.

'You are not a shoemaker by trade?' Mr Lorry said.

'I am not a shoemaker by trade? No, I was not a shoemaker by trade. I—I learnt it here. I taught myself. I asked leave to—' the man rambled.

No time was wasted and arrangements were made to take Mr Manette back to England that night. On the ship, Mr Lorry found that he was seated across the former doctor. Sitting opposite the man who had finally been dug out of his loneliness, he wondered if he would regain his mind.

The year was 1780.

Tellson's Bank by Temple Bar was an old-fashioned place, marked by darkness and ugliness. It was exactly five years ago, when they sent Jerry Cruncher as a messenger.

Jerry Cruncher lived in Whitefriars in a small private lodging with his wife and son. He would yell at his wife for praying and throw his muddy boots at her, calling her names. He would return from the bank with clean boots but often wake up to find them covered with clay. His son—who usually followed his father to work every day—could never understand how his father's fingers were always rusty since bank work didn't involve any iron rust.

One day at the bank, Jerry was given a job to run.

'You know the Old Bailey Courthouse?' one of the clerks said.

'Ye–es, sir,' shot back Jerry. 'I do know the Bailey.'

'Just so. And you know Mr Lorry.'

'I know Mr Lorry, sir, much better than I know the Bailey. Much better,' said Jerry.

So Jerry was to take a note to Mr Lorry at the courthouse, where there was a trial for treason. When the messenger reached the courthouse, he saw Charles Darnay, the young Frenchman who was standing for the trial. Mr Darnay, who had allegedly carried secret information from England to the King of France, was charged for treason.

Though he was ignorant regarding the judicial processes or the legal system, Jerry could make something out from the sight. Mr Lorry and Miss Manette were present in the building. There was a crowd, with eager eyes, inside the court house, curious about the verdict.

With a long, impatient due process of law, Mr Attorney-General was to pass the verdict whether Mr Darnay was innocent. The verdict: evidence proved that he was innocent. CJ Stryver, the defendant's counsel with his assistant Sydney Carton, played key roles in getting the acquittal. Incidentally Carton looked very similar to the accused, Darnay.

Hastily, Mr Lorry wrote a one-word note—ACQUITTED—and handed it over to Jerry.

It was four months after the trial for treason. Mr Lorry, who lived in Clerkenwell, had become a trusted friend of the Manettes who resided near Soho Square. Charles Darnay and Sydney Carton had become regular visitors of the Manettes.

One day, Mr Lorry paid a visit to the Manette residence but the father and daughter were not at home. Instead he talked to Miss Pross, the governess. They chatted on a variety of topics, including the shoemaker's bench, Mr Manette's tools, his knowledge of the person who forced him to be jailed, his recovery, and the suitors who had come for his daughter's hand and so on. Over the years, the doctor had gradually regained his mind.

And when it came to the suitors, Miss Pross would add, 'There never was, nor will be, but one

man worthy of Miss Manette, and that was my brother Solomon, if he hadn't made a mistake in life.'

Solomon was a heartless scoundrel, regretted Miss Pross. Her brother had cut her off everything she owned and left her in extreme poverty.

Later in the day, Mr Darnay visited while the father-daughter duo was back home. When they were chatting about an old tower in London, Mr Darnay mentioned about a carving that read DIG. He was curious and turned to the father.

'Have you seen much of the Tower?'

'Lucie and I have been there; but only casually.'

'I have been there, as you remember. People told me a curious thing when I was there.'

'What was that?' Lucie chipped in.

Darnay began to narrate, 'The floor was examined very carefully under the inscription, and, in the earth beneath a stone, or tile, or some fragment of paving were found along with the ashes of a paper, mingled with the ashes of a small leather case or bag. What the unknown prisoner had written will never be read, but he had written something, and hidden it away to keep it from the jailor.'

Mr Manette was so moved by this story that Lucie thought he had become unconscious.

'Father!' Lucie panicked, 'Are you ill?'

'No, my dear,' Mr Manette said, shaking. 'It's beginning to rain. That startled me. We better go in.'

Mr Carton joined the group soon. He expressed his interest in Lucie indirectly.

Far away in France, Monseigneur, one of the great lords in power, held his fortnightly reception in his grand hotel in Paris. He was in his inner room, his sanctuary of sanctuaries, the Holiest of Holiests to the crowd of worshippers and followers.

Once his carriage ran over and killed a child in a busy and dirty market square. His lack of concern was so clear that he threw a gold coin at the dead child's father. As he left, he barked, 'You dogs! I would ride over anyone willingly and destroy you from the earth.'

On the one hand, the commoners lived in dirty conditions in the busy market area. On the other hand, carriages came whirling by, carrying the Minister, the State-Projector, the Farmer-General, the Doctor, the Lawyer, the Ecclesiastic and other upper-class people in utmost luxury.

Through the country side, the Marquis travelled to the Evrémonde country estate.

'Monsieur Charles, whom I expect; has he arrived from England?' he asked about his nephew to one of his attendants.

'Monseigneur, not yet.'

In the late evening, his nephew who was none other than Charles Darnay arrived with the Manettes. Monseigneur received him in a courtly manner, but they did not shake hands.

Their meeting showed the uncle was not on the best terms with the nephew. In fact, Mr Darnay accused his uncle of having him jailed. When the older man said that it was for family honour, the nephew declared his wish to give up all the privileges and luxuries of aristocratic lifestyle. Also Charles Darnay blamed their family was responsible for the mess France was in.

'This property and France are lost to me,' said the nephew, sadly, 'I give up them.'

Inside the château the next morning, Monseigneur was found murdered. He was stabbed with a note attached to the knife:

'Drive him fast to his tomb. This, from Jacques.'

One year had passed. Mr Charles Darnay was in England. He had settled himself as a teacher of the French language. And he had showed his love for Lucie to her father. Dr Manette was slightly unwilling for some reasons known only to him, but he did not voice his reservations.

Then Mr Darnay, believing the older man deserved more confidence, disclosed that he had been using an assumed name and tried to reveal it.

But the doctor interrupted the young man, 'Tell me when I ask you, not now. If your suit should prosper, if Lucie should love you, you shall tell me on your marriage morning. Do you promise?'

'Willingly,' Mr Darnay agreed happily.

On the same evening while they were drinking, the lawyer CJ Stryver was telling Sydney Carton, his subordinate and Darnay's look alike, that he was planning to marry Lucie Manette. He was describing how suitable he was to women while criticizing his subordinate about being a loser.

The lawyer spoke as if he was doing Lucie a favour by making her his wife, considering the sad life she was sharing with her father. They wished each other goodnight after a suggestion from Mr Stryver.

He recommended, 'Find out some respectable woman with a little property—somebody in the landlady way, or lodging-letting way—and marry her, against a rainy day. That's the kind of thing for you. Now think of it, Sydney.'

The next morning Mr Stryver visited the Manettes, but not before taking some ideas from Mr Lorry who was then at Tellson's. The clerk advised that the lawyer should wait for a while, until he received the acceptance about Lucie's willingness.

In the evening the confusion was confirmed, the Manette was reluctant to Stryver's proposal, much to the annoyance of the lawyer. He could hardly hide his emotion.

'Mr Lorry, you cannot control the mincing vanities and giddiness of empty-headed girls.'

One day in August, Mr Carton was passing by the Manette's house, as always, but that day he decided to drop by and again as always, he was drowned in self-pity when he talked to Lucie. He admitted as well his fascination with the lady and even declared that he would give up his life for her.

One morning Jerry Cruncher was sitting outside Tellson's waiting for the jobs he had to run, should there be any. A march passed on the street. Upon asking, he found that it was the funeral procession of one Roger Cly, convicted at the Old Bailey and executed for spying.

Later in the night, Cruncher scolded his wife for praying. Then he told her he was going out for fishing. However, he was going to the graveyard to dig up Cly's coffin. All along, he had been stealing from graves to cut and sell the body parts to doctors and surgeons.

Unbeknown to him Jerry's son always followed him wherever he went; the boy had never followed his father to the graveyard. That night, he had followed his father without the latter's knowledge, though he came back home running and looking visibly terrified. It was the first time he learnt of his father's second profession.

Back in Paris the next day, Monsieur Defarge was running his business successfully. He had customers at his wine shop as early as six o'clock in the morning. From the street, he took a road-mender named Jacques to the floor where Dr

Manette used to stay. Another three Jacques were present there already and he introduced the road-mender to them.

The road-mender informed the group how one Jacques was executed on the charge of killing the Monseigneur.

It was then apparent that they were revolutionaries, who were working to overthrow the existing aristocracy. Monsieur Defarge was one of the leaders. Even his wife—who was always knitting—was one of them. In reality, she was keeping a register, knitting the names of the enemies to be executed.

One Jacques asked Monsieur Defarge, 'Are you sure that no embarrassment can arise from our manner of keeping the register? Without doubt it is safe, for no one beyond ourselves can decipher it but shall we always be able to decipher it—or, I ought to say, will she?'

'Jacques,' said Defarge, 'If my wife undertook to keep the register in her memory alone, she would not lose a word of it—not a syllable of it. Tell to Madame Defarge.'

A few days later, Defarge got information from a policeman that an English spy named John Barsad was coming to Saint Antoine. Madame Defarge started knitting the name immediately. As predicted, the man arrived, changed as a sympathizer of the revolutionaries. This was not the issue when Madame Defarge talked to him; rather there was a new development.

Barsad, who was aware of Dr Manette's background, narrated that the doctor's daughter was marrying the nephew of Monseigneur. Madame Defarge knitted the name of Charles Darnay after the spy left.

***

Never did the sun go down with a brighter glory on the quiet corner in Soho and it was not without a reason. Lucie was getting married to Darnay the next day. The father and the daughter loved each other very much. Doctor Manette had almost forgotten about the days of prison in Bastille, rather he would narrate happily about his days in France, when Lucie was a baby.

The big day arrived; excitement was in the air. Everything was going fine. The bride and the groom were leaving for a fortnight's trip to Wales for their honeymoon. It was only sad that Miss Pross still thought her brother was the only eligible person for Lucie. Besides, there was a huge change in the behaviour of the bride's father.

Mr Lorry and Miss Pross got really worried when Doctor Manette started shoemaking again. The two of them did try so hard to keep the doctor out of harm's way. They had even taken away the shoemaking tools on the sly and destroyed all of them. They did succeed in the end, as the doctor became normal.

Gradually, days, weeks and months went by. The Darnays were doing fine, except that their first baby boy died soon after birth. But they were blessed with a daughter, whom they named Lucie after her mother.

All these years, Carton had been working for Stryver, and the latter was then married to a widow. Some half-dozen times a year, at most, Carton claimed his privilege of coming in uninvited, and would sit among the Darnays through the evening, as he had once done often.

One night in July 1789, Mr Lorry came in, from Tellson's, and sat himself down by Lucie and her husband.

He said, 'We have been so full of business all day. There is such unrest in Paris, that we have actually a run of confidence upon us! Our customers over there are sending their money and assets to England.'

'You know how gloomy and threatening the sky is,' added Mr Darnay.

Lucie's father joined in then; and turning to Mr Lorry, he said, 'I am going to play backgammon with you, if you like.'

***

In Paris, things were never the same. From Saint Antoine, the Defarges led the people, who were armed with anything they could lay their hands on. Muskets were being distributed as well—so were cartridges, powder, and ball, bars of iron and wood, knives, axes, pikes and what not. And the air was full with battle cry.

'Work, comrades all, work! Work, Jacques One, Jacques Two, Jacques One Thousand, Jacques Two Thousand, Jacques Five-and-Twenty Thousand; in the name of all the Angels or the Devils—which you prefer—work!'

The mob attacked Bastille, the fortress that housed the prison. The first thing Monsieur Defarge did was to locate the cell number One Hundred and Five, North Tower, where Doctor Manette was once held captive. Before the fortress was completely destroyed he got the document that was kept secretly in corner of the cell.

In the meantime, the mob killed the governor; and the violence reached a climax when Madame Defarge beheaded the dead man.

A week had passed after the people attacked Bastille, when one day Monsieur Defarge arrived, breathlessly, at his shop where there had been a gathering.

He shouted, 'Does everybody here recall old Foulon, who told the famished people that they might eat grass, and who died, and went to hell?'

'Everybody!' from all throats.

'The news is of him. He is among us!'

'Among us!' from the throats again. 'And dead?'

'Not dead! He feared us so much—and with reason—that he caused himself to be represented as dead, and had a grand mock-funeral. But they have found him alive, hiding in the country, and have brought him in. Now he is kept at the Hotel de Ville as a prisoner.'

Before long the mob stormed the hotel, grabbed Foulon, stuffed his mouth with grass, and then hung him to death from a lamp post.

The people of Saint Antoine came home satisfied that evening even if they were starving.

Over the next few days, the Evrémonde château was broken, so were other buildings owned by the aristocrats. Destruction continued throughout the country and the revolutionaries were on the winning side.

Three years have passed since the popular revolt had completely overthrown the aristocracy in France. The upheaval was yet to settle. Royalty was gone; it had been besieged in its palace and 'suspended,' when the last tidings came over. It was the August of 1892, and Monseigneur was by this time scattered far and wide.

As was natural, the headquarters and great gathering place of Monseigneur, in London, was Tellson's Bank.

The bank management had decided that Mr Lorry should go to its Paris branch and collect the papers and documents. Charles Darnay tried to stop Mr Lorry from going to the city in such a trying time of his home country but the clerk had finalized his plan to go with Jerry Cruncher as his guard.

In the meantime, while Mr Lorry was talking to Mr Darnay at Tellson's, he got a letter addressed to Marquis St Evrémonde. Nobody knew it was a letter for Mr Darnay who had changed his name after leaving his aristocratic family—and this was his real name. So, he claimed to know the man and volunteered to deliver the letter.

He was taken aback completely when he read the letter. It was from one of his former attendants, Gabelle, who had been jailed by the revolutionaries. The prisoner, who was the last of the important persons related to the aristocrats, had written for his life.

Though initially Darnay was advising Mr Lorry against travelling to France, then it was him who had to go first.

He found out the hard way that it was not easy to travel in France those days. Every town-gate and village taxing-house had its band of citizen-patriots or the revolutionaries. They stood guard attentively, with their muskets, and frisked all the people who were going in both directions.

Finally when he reached Paris, he was arrested immediately and was going to be put away in a prison right away.

He protested, 'Under what law, and for what offence?'

The officer looked up from his slip of paper, 'We have new laws, Evrémonde, and new offences, since you were here.'

Darnay tried to argue, but he was cut short; the other man replied steadfastly, 'Emigrants have no rights, Evrémonde.'

When Defarge arrived a moment later, he argued again but in vain. And the worst came when he was thrown in a cell for solitary confinement. He could realize why and how Dr Manette had taken to shoemaking.

***

Mr Lorry had reached Paris in the Saint Germain Quarter. He was glad no one close to him was hurt, when chaos and unrest filled the French air. One day Lucie, Dr Manette and Miss Pross arrived at his door, breathless and worried.

He was taken back, 'What is the matter? Lucie! Manette! What has happened?'

'Charles,' replied his wife.

'What of Charles?'

'Here.'

'Here, in Paris?'

'He has been here some days—three or four—I don't know how many—but he was stopped at the barrier, and sent to prison,' continued Charles's wife excitedly.

The situation was too grave, more bothered by the knowledge that the protestors were killing all the prisoners. Fortunately, Dr Manette convinced the crowd who were heading to Bastille, telling them that he was once a prisoner during the previous regime. Lucie was with Mr Lorry, while Jerry Cruncher guarded the place.

Further, luck was on their side when the bank clerk and the lady met Monsieur Defarge, who told them that Darnay was safe. The only caveat was neither Dr Manette nor Darnay were allowed to leave the prison.

Dr Manette did not return until the morning of the fourth day of his absence. But it had been a blessing in disguise. In this short period, eleven hundred defenceless prisoners of both sexes and all ages had been killed by the populace. The doctor's presence in the prison ensured that Darnay was unharmed. Besides, he used his personal influence so wisely, that he was soon the inspecting physician of the prison.

Soon, the agitation and subsequent condition promised a new era—the king was tried, doomed, and killed. It was time for the declaration of the Republic of Liberty, Equality and Fraternity.

One year and three months passed as Lucie waited for the release of her husband. Her father brought a piece of news one evening.

He told her, 'My dear, there is an upper window in the prison, to which Charles can sometimes gain access at three in the afternoon. When he can get to it he might see you in the street, if you stood in a certain place that I can show you. But you will not be able to see him, my poor child.'

'Oh, show me the place, my father, and I will go there every day.'

From that day, she stood for two hours every day, from two o'clock to four o'clock, come rain or shine.

Finally, to stand for a trial, Darnay's name appeared in the list of prisoners—made by the terrible tribunal of five judges, a public prosecutor and a determined jury, which sat every day. The trial was scheduled for the following day.

'Take off his head!' cried the audience. 'An enemy to the Republic!'

As always the crowd was baying for the prisoners' blood. However, the charges against Darnay were minimal compared to the privileges he possessed. For instance, he belonged to the aristocratic family but he had nothing to do with any of the family members. He was married to the daughter of a popular doctor, who also testified on his behalf. Besides, he had been tried by both the governments of France and England. Unsurprisingly he was acquitted.

But the excitement was short-lived.

The next day, Miss Pross and Jerry Cruncher had gone shopping. Four rough men in red caps, armed with sabres and pistols, knocked on the door.

'The Citizen Evremonde, called Darnay,' said the first.

'Who seeks him?' asked Darnay.

'I seek him. We seek him. I know you, Evrémonde; I saw you before the Tribunal today. You are again the prisoner of the Republic.'

Apparently, Monsieur Defarge, Madame Defarge and one unamed person had fresh charges against him. Dr Manette tried to interrupt but he was cut short.

One of the men said, 'Citizen Doctor, ask no more. If the Republic demands sacrifices from you, without doubt you as a good patriot will be happy to make them. The Republic goes before all. The people are supreme. Evremonde, we are pressed.'

The trial again was scheduled for the next day. Outside when Miss Pross and Jerry were shopping, the lady ran into her long lost brother, Solomon, disguised. Incidentally he was the alleged English spy, John Barsad, who once came to Defarge's wine shop.

'Oh, Solomon, dear Solomon!' said Miss Pross.

'Don't call me Solomon. Do you want me to die?' replied the man, in a secret, frightened way.

Jerry, too had recognized Miss Pross' brother as the witness who accused Charles Darnay many years ago.

Accidentally, the three of them met Sydney Carton, who was in Paris for a day, and he also knew the spy. Carton threatened to reveal Solomon's true identity to the French revolutionaries if John Barsad did not come to Tellson's at once. He also charged that he had seen Barsad talking to another spy, Robert Cly, though the latter objected, saying Cly was dead a long time ago. Then Jerry said the second spy was alive because he had seen the coffin and there was no Cly in it!

The men met at Tellson's and there was only one plan: to get Darnay out of the prison. And Barsad was the only person who could help because he had access to the prison. Before they parted, Mr Lorry scolded Jerry for being a grave robber; he also told him that this might cost him his job.

The day of the second trial arrived. When the list of juries came out, many people were taken aback. It included Ernest Defarge, Therese Defarge and Jacques Three of St Antoine, and most surprisingly, Dr Manette. The doctor objected but Monsieur Defarge explained the document he had unearthed from the doctor's prison cell a long time ago.

In the document, the doctor had denounced Darnay's father and uncle for his misfortune. It also served as an evidence as to how the Evrémonde brothers had been so cruel in dealing with the peasants during their rule. And they had already incriminated Dr Manette for lack of cooperation. It was wrong and their acts had to be criticized. Then Darnay was found answerable because he was their heir, regardless of any other fact.

The jury sentenced Charles Darnay to death. He was going to be executed along with fifty-two other convicts the next day.

With the help of John Barsad, Carton slipped into the prison and met Darnay, who had almost resigned himself to death. Carton was a look-alike and he was going to take the place of the condemned Frenchman. He drugged Darnay and took his place, while Mr Barsad dragged out the latter.

Before long, Mr Lorry, Dr Manette, Lucie and her daughter boarded a carriage—with a half-conscious Darnay, who was now given the name of Carton and one of his pockets was stuffed with identification papers, which originally belonged to Carton, the sacrificial hero. Mr Cruncher and Miss Pross were to leave separately later in the day. The carriage left Paris as quickly as possible. And finally they were all free!

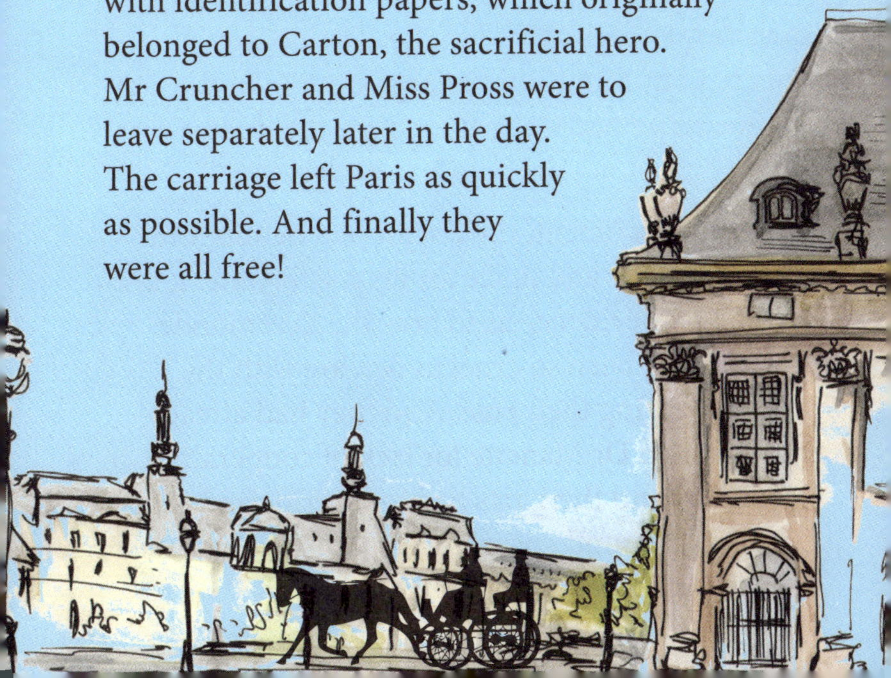

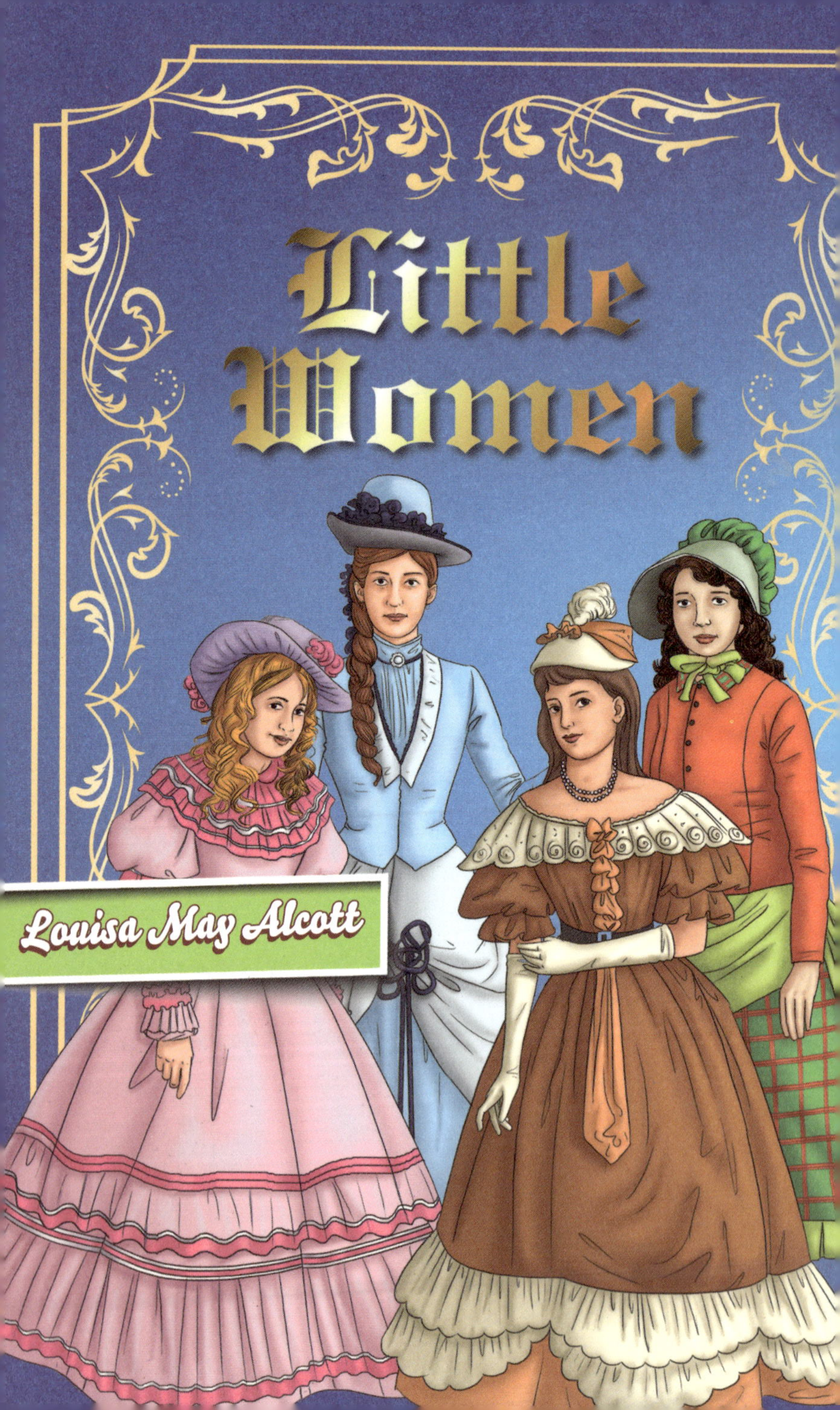
Little Women
Louisa May Alcott

On a cold December evening in a small, quiet town, four sisters were sitting around the fireplace in their parlour and feeling quite sad.

'Christmas won't be Christmas without any presents,' said Jo.

'It's so bad to be poor!' said Meg.

'I don't think it's fair for some girls to have plenty of pretty things, and other girls nothing at all,' said little Amy.

'We've got Father and Mother, and each other,' said Beth contentedly.

The March family used to be wealthy, but had lost everything. Their father, Mr March, was away at war, and their mother, who they affectionately called Marmee, didn't want to waste money that year.

Meg was sixteen and the oldest of the four. She was the prettiest of all her sisters and liked taking care of the household. Jo was the second oldest at fifteen. She loved reading and writing and was a bit of a tomboy. Beth was thirteen and very shy. She liked playing the piano and playing with kittens. Amy was twelve and the artist of the lot. Being the youngest, she was a little self-centred and spoilt.

After thinking of all the presents they would buy for themselves, the girls changed their minds. They would instead buy presents for their mother. After much discussion the gift items were finalized: a pair of gloves, shoes, a handkerchief and perfume.

When their father had lost all his money in trying to help a friend, the two older girls begged their parents to let them start working and take care of themselves. Meg worked as a nursery governess and Jo worked with Aunt March, an old and lame relative. Though the old lady didn't much like the March family, because they had refused her help in the past, she had a special liking for Jo and her blunt ways.

Jo liked working at Aunt March's mostly because of her large library, which Jo searched every time her aunt took a nap.

Beth was so shy that she didn't go to school, and instead stayed home to do housework and look after her doll collection. She cried every once in a while because she loved music but didn't have a good piano to play on.

Amy went to school, but her biggest problem was her nose. It was somewhat flat and she blamed Jo for it. When she was a baby, Jo had dropped her on her face, and she thought that the fall was the cause of her troubles. She was a good artist and constantly drew long pointy noses to calm herself. Unlike Beth, she liked being social and was popular at school.

The four girls all got along, well most of the time, but Meg took special care of Amy, while Jo took special care of Beth.

On Christmas day, the girls were in for a surprise. They each found a book under their pillows when they woke up! When Meg and Jo ran to thank Marmee for their gifts, the mother wasn't around. Their housekeeper, Hannah, told the girls that Marmee had gone out to help a starving family.

An hour later Marmee came into the kitchen. 'Merry Christmas, Marmee! Thank you for our books! We'll read them every day!' they all yelled in chorus.

'Merry Christmas little daughters,' Marmee said, then asked them to not eat breakfast.

The girls were confused, and hungry. Marmee instructed them to give their breakfast as a Christmas present to the starving family. They agreed, and spent a nice day with their less fortunate neighbours.

They didn't know that there would be a surprise at dinnertime too!

The dining table was set with fresh flowers and dishes were filled with vanilla and strawberry ice cream, cake, fruit and French bonbons. Their neighbour, Mr Laurence, came to know of the good deed they had done that day and wanted to reward them with a feast of their own. The girls only knew him as the old man who lived in the big house next door who did not let his grandson talk to them. Jo then decided that the Marches would have to make an effort to know the Laurences.

A few days later, Jo was reading a book in the attic and crying over it while eating apples. Her pet rat, Scrabble, was keeping her company. Meg called her from downstairs. The two elder sisters had been invited to a New Year's Eve party by Sallie Gardiner, Meg's friend.

'What shall we wear?' asked Meg, even though they both knew they had only one party dress each. Jo's dress had a burn mark at the back, but she hadn't had time to fix it. 'You must sit still all you can and keep your back out of sight. The front is all right,' said Meg.

When the day came, the two older sisters nervously made their way to Sallie's house. Meg immediately met Sallie and began chatting with her. Jo didn't want to join in, so she stood around feeling awkward. Not wanting people to come talk to her, she hid in a corner behind a curtain.

But she wasn't alone. Standing there with her was Mr Laurence's grandson.

'My first name is Theodore, but I don't like it, for the fellows called me Dora, so I made them say Laurie instead.'

'I hate my name, too, so sentimental! I wish everyone would say Jo instead of Josephine. How did you make the boys stop calling you Dora?'

'I thrashed them.'

They thought of dancing, but didn't want to join the others, so Laurie taught Jo the polka in a corridor. Jo went to look for Meg after the dance and found her sitting on a sofa holding her foot.

'I've sprained my ankle. That stupid high heel turned and gave me a sad wrench. It aches so, I can hardly stand, and I don't know how I'm ever going to get home,' she said, rocking to and fro in pain.

Thankfully Laurie came to the rescue and offered them a ride home in his carriage.

As it was nearing the end of winter, Jo was pushing snow off the pathways in the garden, which separated their house from the Laurences'. Theirs was an old brown house, while the Laurences' was a high building. The girls had always wondered what it was like inside the mansion, all mysterious and elegant and richly furnished. Jo also wondered if Laurie was lonely. She had seen him watching her sisters and her playing in the garden, and thought that he would like to play with them.

When she saw him this time at the window, she threw a snowball at him.

'How do you do? Are you sick?'

Laurie opened the window, and said hoarsely, 'I've had a bad cold, and been shut up a week.'

Jo took some blancmange and a few of Beth's kittens next door to cheer him up. She talked and talked all afternoon and Laurie was quite amused. He told her why he always watched them play.

'When I'm alone up here, I can't help looking over at your house, you always seem to be having such good times. I can't help watching it. I haven't got my mother, you know.'

Jo felt sorry for him and said that he could come and play with them whenever he felt like.

That afternoon, she met Old Mr Laurence. He invited her to have tea with them and Jo readily agreed. She saw a piano in the drawing room. She asked Laurie to play it for her, but his grandfather became angry and said that it was time for her to go home.

'He doesn't like to hear me play,' Laurie said.

'Why not?'

'I'll tell you some day.'

After that day the sisters spent more and more time with the Laurences. Meg loved the gardens, Amy the art. Beth loved the grand piano, but she was a bit scared of Old Mr Laurence.

When he learned that Beth was scared of him, he told Marmee, 'The boy neglects his music now, but the piano needs to be used. Wouldn't some of your girls like to run over, and practise on it now and then, just to keep it in tune, you know, ma'am?'

Beth was delighted and from then on went to the Laurences' house during the day to play on the piano. She reminded Old Mr Laurence of his granddaughter who had passed away; the piano used to belong to her.

Beth made him a pair of brown slippers in gratitude. She took them into the old man's study with Laurie's help, then waited to see how the old man would like them. When Mr Laurence found the slippers, he had his granddaughter's piano sent to the March's house. Beth went to thank him, but no words came out. Instead, she kissed him on the cheek. He was so touched by this that he began to like the March girls even more.

A few months passed and it became warm again. Summer was here. Meg had lost a pair of gloves a few weeks ago, but someone had put one of them in the post box with a note.

'Miss Meg March, one letter and a glove,' said Beth, delivering the articles to her sister, who sat near her mother, stitching wristbands.

The note was a translation of a German song by Mr Brooke, Laurie's tutor. Meg didn't think anything of it, though Marmee believed that Mr Brooke was trying to court Meg.

Jo had a letter from Laurie inviting the girls to a picnic the next day with some of his friends and Mr Brooke. There would be rowing and croquet and a lunch. On the day of the picnic, Laurie and Jo rowed one boat, while Meg sat facing Mr Brooke.

Mr Brooke was a serious, silent young man, with handsome brown eyes and a pleasant voice. Meg liked his quiet ways. He never talked to her much, but he looked at her a lot. One of Laurie's friends found out that Meg was a governess and was very rude to her because of that. But Mr Brooke defended Meg, calling her an independent young lady.

When the autumn came, Jo was very busy writing stories. She'd written two manuscripts and sneaked out of the house to send them to the local newspaper. She deposited them at the desk and stepped out carefully. But she couldn't keep the secret for long because Laurie met her on the road.

Laurie was proud of her and offered to give her some information.

'I know where Meg's glove is,' Laurie said.

'Is that all?' said Jo, looking disappointed.

It wasn't. Laurie told Jo that Mr Brooke kept Meg's other glove in his pocket all the time. Jo was not happy with this information because she didn't want Meg to be married so soon.

A few days later the paper with Jo's stories came in. She read it aloud to her family.

'Who wrote it?' asked Beth, who had caught a glimpse of the excitement on Jo's face.

Jo said in a loud voice, 'Your sister.'

'You?' cried Meg, dropping her work.

'It's very good,' said Amy critically.

Jo wasn't paid for her first stories, but would be paid for the next ones she wrote. She felt very proud of herself indeed.

In November that year, Marmee received a telegram, telling her that Mr March was unwell. She had to leave the house to take care of him. They were short of money for the trip, so Marmee asked Aunt March for some. But Jo had other plans.

She sneaked out when nobody was looking and went to a barber. She had her long dark hair cut off and earned $25 for it.

'Your hair! Your beautiful hair!'

'Oh, Jo, how could you? Your one beauty.'

'My dear girl, there was no need of this.'

'She doesn't look like my Jo any more, but I love her dearly for it!'

'I hadn't the least idea of selling my hair at first, but as I went along I kept thinking what I could do, and feeling as if I'd like to dive into some of the rich stores and help myself. In a barber's window I saw tails of hair with the prices marked, and one black tail, not so thick as mine, was forty dollars. It came to me all of a sudden that I had one thing to make money out of, and without stopping to think, I walked in, asked if they bought hair, and what they would give for mine,' said Jo.

Jo said that it didn't matter and she didn't care what she looked like. The money was more important. That night, she cried herself to sleep.

While Marmee was away, the girls wrote letters to her every day. She told them not to forget the poor family that they'd helped last Christmas. The girls listened, but only Beth went to visit the family every day.

On one visit, she returned home with some bad news. 'Mrs Hummel's baby died in my lap before she got home,' said Beth. 'It had scarlet fever!'

A couple of days later, Beth felt ill, so Hannah called for Dr Bangs to check her out. When he did, he found that Beth had the fever. Meg and Jo were safe, because they had had it before, but Amy was not, so she was sent to live with Aunt March for a few days until Beth was cured.

Amy didn't want to go, but Laurie managed to convince her to go quietly, promising that he would visit her every day.

'She is lying down on Mother's bed, and feels better. The baby's death troubled her, but I dare say she has only got cold. Hannah says she thinks so, but she looks worried, and that makes me restless,' said Meg.

'What a trying world it is!' said Jo, curling up her hair in a irritable way. 'No sooner do we get out of one trouble than down comes another. There doesn't seem to be anything to hold on to when Mother's gone, so I'm all at sea.'

'Well, don't make a porcupine of yourself, it isn't becoming. Settle your wig, Jo, and tell me if I shall telegraph to your mother, or do anything?' asked Laurie, who never had been reconciled to the loss of his friend's one beauty.

Beth got so sick that the girls thought of calling Marmee back. Jo cried in Laurie's arms that Beth would die and Marmee wouldn't be at home. He assured her that he had already sent Marmee a telegram.

On one dark night, Beth was still, and Jo thought she would die. She whispered her goodbyes.

'Goodbye, my Beth. Goodbye!'

Hannah, who was sleeping near Beth woke up at that moment and reached to feel Beth's temperature.

'The fever's gone. She's sleeping normally and breathing easily. My goodness me!'

'It looks like a fairy world,' said Meg, smiling to herself, as she stood behind the curtain, watching the shining sight.

'Hark!' said Jo, starting to her feet.

Yes, there was a sound of bells at the door below, a cry from Hannah, and then Laurie's voice saying in a joyful whisper, 'Girls, she's come! She's come!'

In the Christmas of that year Mr March had written that he would be coming home soon. Beth was feeling good that day, so she stood by the window wrapped in her new red shawl and watched as Laurie and Jo built her a snow princess.

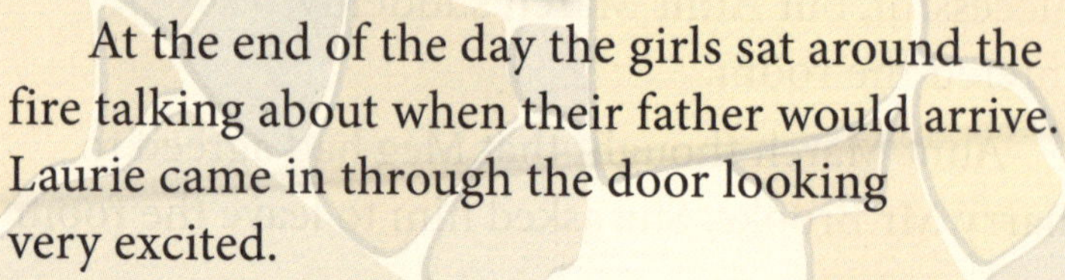

At the end of the day the girls sat around the fire talking about when their father would arrive. Laurie came in through the door looking very excited.

'And here's another present for the March family,' he said, stepping aside.

Behind him was a tall man, muffled up the eyes, leaning on the arm of another tall man. For a few minutes, there was commotion as the girls ran to hug their father.

In the commotion, Mr Brooke, who was helping Mr March, kissed Meg without thinking.

That evening the girls sat with their father after dinner as he told how proud he was of them.

***

Meg was beginning to have feelings for Mr Brooke, and blushed whenever his name was mentioned. She knew her parents thought that she was too young to be married, so she'd planned a speech in which she would reject him.

Mr Brooke had come to the March's house to retrieve his umbrella. Meg asked him to wait in the parlour while she called her parents, but Mr Brooke had finally found his chance to propose. She tried rejecting him and was almost successful, but Aunt March suddenly entered the room.

Aunt March thought that Meg had agreed to marry Mr Brooke. She asked him to leave the room and then lectured Meg on how she was supposed to find a rich husband and not a tutor. 'Tell me, do you mean to marry this Cook? If you do, not one penny of my money ever goes to you. Remember that, and be a sensible girl,' said the old lady.

'I shall marry whom I please, Aunt March, and you can leave your money to anyone you like,' she said.

Mr Brooke came back and asked her if she would marry him in a few years. Meg said yes.

***

Three years passed, and Meg's wedding was due. Mr March and Mr Brooke had gone back to the war, but it had ended and they would soon be home.

In those years that passed, Meg had learned how to keep a house, Jo had continued writing stories and Amy had become Aunt March's caretaker. Laurie was away at college.

One day a tall, broad-shouldered young man, with short hair, a felt hat and a flyaway coat came walking to their door. It was Laurie, all grown up, with a gift for Meg. He and Jo talked about Meg's wedding and Jo begged him not to make her laugh during the ceremony.

'You are a mere infant, but you'll go next, Jo, and we'll be left feeling sad,' said Laurie, shaking his head.

'Nobody will want me, and that's a good thing,' said Jo.

'You won't give anyone a chance,' said Laurie, blushing.

The June wedding was small, but filled with roses and the people the family loved. The girls were dressed in their summer best. Meg looked like a rose herself in the dress she had made. The only ornaments she wore were lilies in her hair. Jo looked much softer. Her wild curls had tamed into long waves that suited her very well. Beth had been becoming more and more weak over the years and was now pale and slender. Amy had grown into a beautiful young woman and at sixteen, she held herself with grace. The three sisters were in dresses of silver grey and wore roses in their hair.

Meg left the family house after the celebration.

'Thank you all for my happy wedding day. Goodbye, goodbye!'

Amy was learning the difficult lesson that talent did not mean genius. She spent a lot of time working on her art and taking art classes and tried her hand at every kind of art possible to see if there was one style she could excel in. She also hadn't lost her sociable personality and tried to throw parties that she couldn't afford so that she could impress her friends.

Jo kept on at her writing. Every few weeks she would shut herself up in her room, put on her writing clothes and lose herself in the novel she was working on.

She had just come out of one of the periods of locking herself up when she had the chance to attend a People's course on the Pyramids. She found herself sitting next to a studious-looking boy who was reading a paper with great interest. It was a silly story that he was reading, one that Jo would never have written herself. But she also saw that the newspaper the story was in was offering a $100 prize for stories just like that one.

The next day, Jo got into one of her writing fits again and wrote out a story for the competition. She posted it and then had to wait six weeks for a response.

Six weeks was a long time to wait, and a still longer time to keep a secret, but Jo did both. She was just beginning to give up all hope of winning, when a letter arrived that contained a cheque for $100. She read the encouraging letter from the publisher and began to cry.

'What will you do with such a fortune?' asked Amy.

'Send Beth and Mother to the seaside for a month or two,' answered Jo promptly.

Jo kept on working on stories to get more $100 cheques. She earned several that year. 'The Duke's Daughter' paid the butcher's bill, 'A Phantom Hand' bought a new carpet, and the 'Curse of the Coventrys' bought groceries and gowns.

Meanwhile, Meg and Mr Brooke were learning how to be a married couple. She was enthusiastic about being a good housekeeper and was mostly careful with money because they were poor. They had occasional fights like all married couples, but on the whole were quite happy. Meg was soon pregnant and gave birth to twins: John Laurence and Margaret, who they nicknamed Demi and Daisy.

Amy, in turn, was to leave for Europe with an aunt and was very excited at the prospect.

***

'Jo, I'm anxious about Beth.'

'Why, Mother, she has seemed unusually well since the babies came.'

Jo felt that it was natural for Beth to feel a bit low with longing. Beth was now eighteen and not a child, even though the family still treated her as one. Jo suspected that maybe Beth was growing to love Laurie.

Laurie was in the habit of falling in love with a new girl every week. But Jo was afraid that these were just pastimes, and the one he really loved was her. She decided to go to New York for a while to live with a lady named Mrs Kirke who was looking for a young person who could stay with them and teach her children how to sew. While she was away, she hoped that Beth and Laurie would become close.

On the day she left home, she told Beth, 'Look after my boy.' But when Laurie said goodbye, he said, 'It's of no use, Jo. My eye is on you, so be careful, or I'll come and bring you home.'

In New York, Jo met another boarder at Mrs Kirke's. He was a German professor named Frederick Bhaer who was about forty years old. They became friends after she mended some of his clothes and he began teaching her German.

She got a job at *The Weekly Volcano* to write silly stories like the ones she had written before. She didn't like writing them, but was paid a lot of money and so continued. She began to hate herself more and more because of the philosophical discussions she had with Mr Bhaer. He was involved with the highest level of thinking, while she wrote for the lowest level.

When Mr Bhaer found out that she wrote those stories, she was so ashamed that she stopped that very day.

Soon, the year was up and it was time for Jo to return home. She told Mr Bhaer, 'Now, Sir, you won't forget to come and see us, if you ever travel our way, will you? I'll never forgive you if you do, for I want them all to know my friend.'

'Do you? Shall I come?' he asked eagerly.

After she'd gone, Bhaer felt sad and tried to tell himself that Jo was not for him.

Amy was still in Europe when Laurie graduated, but the rest of the Marches were there

with him that day. He'd kept his eyes on Jo after the ceremony and she knew the time was coming when he would declare his intentions for her. It made her very uncomfortable.

She met him as usual the next day, but tried to keep her distance. When she saw him looking at her with an expectant expression all she could say was, 'Please, don't.' But Laurie wouldn't listen.

'I've loved you ever since I've known you, Jo. I've tried to show it, but you wouldn't let me. Now I'm going to make you hear, and give me an answer, for I can't go on so any longer.'

Jo had to tell him.

'You're a great deal too good for me, and I'm so grateful to you, and so proud and fond of you. I don't know why I can't love you as you want me to. I've tried, but I can't change the feeling, and it would be a lie to say I do when I don't.'

Laurie was so unhappy that he lay on the ground, not knowing what to do with himself.

'You know it's impossible for people to make themselves love other people if they don't,' Jo said sadly, as she softly patted his shoulder.

Laurie returned home and played the piano that night.

'That's very fine, I dare say, but it's sad enough to make one cry. Give us something gayer, lad,' said Mr Laurence, whose kind old heart was full of sympathy, which he desired to show but knew not how.

Laurie stayed sad for days until Mr Laurence, who knew what happened between the two youngsters, suggested that Laurie accompany him on a trip to Europe.

'Take it like a man, and don't do anything rash, for God's sake. Why not go abroad, as you planned?'

'I can't.'

'But you've been wild to go, and I promised you should when you got through college.'

'Ah, but I didn't mean to go alone!' and Laurie walked fast through the room with an expression which it was well his grandfather did not see.

'I don't ask you to go alone. There's someone ready and glad to go with you, anywhere in the world.'

'Who, Sir?' stopping to listen.

'Myself.'

And so Laurie went along sadly.

On Jo's return, she saw that Beth had become paler and thinner. She planned a trip with her to

the seaside in the hope that Beth would feel better, but it didn't work. During the trip, Beth told her that she didn't think she would live for very long. When they returned, Marmee and Mr March saw for themselves that Beth was losing hope.

While it was dark and painful at the March's house, Amy was having the time of her life in France. She'd met Laurie and saw that he was depressed so tried to cheer him up.

'Here are your flowers. I arranged them myself, remembering that you didn't like what Hannah calls a "sot-bookay"' said Laurie, handing her a delicate nosegay, in a holder that she had long coveted as she daily passed it in Cardiglia's window.

'How kind you are!' she exclaimed gratefully. 'If I'd known you were coming I'd have had something ready for you today, though not as pretty as this, I'm afraid.'

'Thank you. It isn't what it should be, but you have improved it,' he added, as she snapped the silver bracelet on her wrist.

'Please don't.'

'I thought you liked that sort of thing.'

'Not from you, it doesn't sound natural, and I like your old bluntness better.'

'I'm glad of it,' he said, with a look of relief, then buttoned her gloves for her, and asked if his tie was straight, just as he used to do when they went to parties together at home.

They had become close friends.

Beth's health continued to get so worse she couldn't get out of bed. The Marches set up a room for her in which they placed her beloved piano, Amy's drawings,

flowers and her kittens. Meg brought the twins over to bring some sunshine into Beth's world. They watched as she got weaker and weaker.

One day, she said to Jo, 'I know it cannot, and I don't fear death any longer. You must take my place, Jo, and be everything to Father and Mother when I'm gone.'

'I'll try, Beth,' said Jo.

She continued to fade through the spring, and then, when summer came, Beth said goodbye.

Amy and Laurie found out about Beth's death at the same time, and Laurie rushed to Amy's side to comfort her. They spent more and more time together, each beginning to love the other.

'Do you care to dance?' Laurie asked Amy.

'One usually does at a ball.'

Her amazed look and quick answer caused Laurie to repair his error as fast as possible.

'I meant the first dance. May I have the honour?'

'I can give you one if I put off the Count.'

One day, when they were rowing a boat on a river, Amy said, 'How well we pull together, don't we?'

'So well that I wish we might always pull in the same boat. Will you, Amy?' asked Laurie very tenderly.

'Yes, Laurie.'

They were married in Europe and returned home to meet their families. While the Marches were celebrating the wedding, Mr Bhaer paid them a visit and was invited to join in the festivities.

'I suspect that is a wise man,' said Mr March, with satisfaction, from the hearthrug, after the last guest had gone.

'I know he is a good one,' said Mrs March, with decided approval, as she wound up the clock.

'I thought you'd like him,' was all Jo said, as she slipped away to her bed.

After two weeks of meeting Mr Bhaer every day, Jo hadn't seen him for three days. She wondered what happened to him. She left the house to run some errands with the hope that she would meet him somewhere in the street. It started to rain as she left the house, but she didn't take her umbrella.

While crossing the street she bumped into a man. It was Mr Bhaer.

He'd had some business in town and was soon heading to the West for a job. Jo was so saddened by this that she started to cry. Mr Bhaer saw the tear drops on her cheeks, though she turned her head away. The sight seemed to touch him very much, for suddenly bending down, he asked, 'Heart's dearest, why do you cry?'

'Because you are going away.'

'Jo, I have nothing but much love to give you. I waited to be sure that I was something more than a friend. Am I?'

'Oh, yes!' said Jo.

Jo and Mr Bhaer spent a year apart before they could marry. Aunt March passed away and handed down her mansion to Jo, out of which Jo made a school. In October, the Marches, Brookes, Laurences and Bhaers gathered together for Marmee's sixtieth birthday. While Jo was planning her next novel, Amy was worried about her little daughter, Beth, who was ill. But the family was all together and that made the occasion a happy one.

Touched to the heart, Mrs March could only stretch out her arms, as if to gather children and grandchildren to herself, and say, with face and voice full of motherly love, gratitude, and humility...

'Oh, my girls, however long you may live, I never can wish you a greater happiness than this!'

Black Beauty
The Autobiography of a Horse
Anna Sewell

The first place that I remember living in was a pleasant meadow with a pond of clear water. I couldn't eat grass, so I drank my mother's milk. In the daytime I ran with her, and at night I lay down next to her to sleep. In the summer we stood near the pond under the trees, and when it was cold we lived in a warm shed.

There were six other young colts in the meadow and they were older than me. We used to play together, galloping around the field. Sometimes we would bite and kick.

One day, my mother said to me, 'The colts who live here are very nice colts, but they are cart-horse colts, and they have no manners. Your father and grandfather won many races and I'm sure you've never seen your grandmother or I kick or bite. I hope you will grow up gentle and good.'

I have never forgotten my mother's advice. Her name was Duchess, but my master called her Pet.

Our master was a good kind man. When my mother saw him at the gate she would neigh with joy and trot up to him. He would stroke her and say, 'Well, old Pet, and how is your little Darkie?' I was a dull black, so he called me Darkie. All the horses would come to him, but I think we were his favourites.

I was two years old when I watched my first foxhunt. First I saw the hounds, running through the fields of wheat.

'They have found a hare,' said my mother, 'and if they come this way we shall see the hunt.'

After them came a number of men on horseback, all galloping as fast as they could. The hare was spotted and in the confusion two horses fell down, one in a stream, the other on the hard ground. One of the riders was getting out of the water covered with mud, the other lay quite still.

'His neck is broken,' said my mother.

While my mother was saying this, the other colts and I stood and looked on. Many of the riders had gone to the young man but my master was the first to raise him up. There was no noise now; even the dogs were quiet, and seemed to know that something was wrong. They carried him to our master's house. I heard afterwards that it was the squire's only son, a fine tall young man, and the pride of his family.

When Bond, the farrier, came to look at the black horse that lay crying on the grass, he felt him all over, and shook his head; one of his legs was broken. Then someone ran to our master's house and came back with a gun. There was a loud bang and a scream, and then all was still; the black horse didn't move anymore.

My mother seemed much troubled; she said she had known that horse for years, and that his name was Rob Roy; he was a good horse, and there was no vice in him. She never would go to that part of the field afterwards.

Not many days after, we heard the church-bell tolling for a long time, and coaches drawn by black horses. They were carrying the young man to the churchyard to bury him. What they did with Rob Roy I never knew but it was all for one little hare.

When I was four years old, my coat had grown fine and soft, and was bright black. I had one white foot and a pretty white star on my forehead. I was thought to be very good looking. Squire Gordon came to look at me one day and

said, 'When he has been well broken in he will do very well.'

Breaking in means to teach a horse to wear a saddle and bridle, how to carry a rider and how to behave. I had to learn how to wear a bit in my mouth, a saddle, blinkers and iron shoes, all of which were very uncomfortable. Especially the bit, which was a piece of cold steel that was pushed between my teeth and was attached to the reins.

My master often drove me in double harness, with my mother because she was steady and could teach me how to go better than a strange horse. She told me the better I behaved the better I should be treated, and that it was wisest always to do my best to please my master.

'I hope you will fall into good hands, but a horse never knows who may buy him, or who may drive him; it is all a chance for us but still I say, do your best wherever it is, and keep up your good name.'

In early May that year, my master said, 'Goodbye, Darkie; be a good horse and always do your best,' and I left my first home. I was taken to a roomy stable and was put in a box stall. The horse that was put into it was not tied up, but left loose, to do as he liked. It is a great thing to have a box stall. It was clean, sweet, and airy.

In the stall next to mine stood a little fat grey pony, with a thick mane and tail, a very pretty head, and a pert little nose. I put my head up to the iron rails at the top of my box, and said, 'How do you do? What is your name?'

He turned round as far as his halter would allow, held up his head, and said, 'My name is Merrylegs. I carry the young ladies on my back, and sometimes I take our mistress out in the low cart. They think a great deal of me, and so does James. Are you going to live next door to me in the box?'

I said, 'Yes.'

'Well, then,' he said, 'I hope you are good-tempered; I do not like any one next door who bites'. Just then a horse's head looked over from the stall beyond; the ears were laid back, and the eye looked rather ill-tempered. This was a tall chestnut mare, with a long handsome neck; she looked across to me and said, 'So it is you who have turned me out of my box.'

'I beg your pardon,' I said, 'I have turned no one out; the man who brought me put me here, and I had nothing to do with it.'

'Well,' she said, 'we shall see' and I talked no more. In the afternoon, when she went out, Merrylegs told me all about it.

'The thing is this,' said Merrylegs, 'Ginger has a habit of biting and snapping; that is why they call her Ginger, and when she was in the box-stall, she used to snap very much. One day she bit James in the arm and made it bleed, and so Miss Flora and Miss Jessie, who are very fond of me, were afraid to come into the stable.'

I told him I never bit anything but grass, hay and corn, and could not think what pleasure Ginger found it.

'Well, I don't think she does find pleasure,' says Merrylegs, 'it is just a bad habit; she says no one was ever kind to her, and why should she not bite?'

The name of the coachman was John Manly; he had a wife and one child, and lived in the coachman's cottage, near the stables. The next morning he took me into the yard and gave me a good grooming. After breakfast he came and fitted me with a saddle and bridle. He rode me first slowly, then a trot, then a canter, and when we were on open ground, he gave me a light touch with his whip, and we had a splendid gallop.

As we came back through the park we met my master and his wife taking a walk; they stopped, and John jumped off.

'Well, John, how does he go?'

'First rate, sir,' said John, 'he is as fleet as a deer, and has a fine spirit, too but the lightest touch of the rein will guide him.'

'That's well,' said the squire, 'I will try him myself tomorrow.'

The next day I was brought up for my master. I remembered my mother's counsel and my good old master's, and I tried to do exactly what he wanted me to do. I found he was a very good rider, and thoughtful for his horse, too. When he came home, the lady was at the hall door as he rode up. 'Well, my dear,' she said, 'how do you like him?'

'He is exactly what John said,' he replied, 'a pleasanter creature I never wish to climb. What shall we call him?'

She said, 'He is really quite a beauty, and he has such a sweet, good-tempered face and such a fine, intelligent eye—what do you say to calling him "Black Beauty"?'

'Black Beauty—why, yes, I think that is a very good name. If you like, it shall be his name'; and so it was.

When John went into the stable, he told the stable boy my new name. They both laughed, and James said, 'If it was not for bringing back the past, I should have named him Rob Roy, for I never saw two horses more alike.'

'That's no wonder,' said John, 'didn't you know that Farmer Grey's old Duchess was the mother of them both?'

I had never heard that before; and so poor Rob Roy who was killed at that hunt was my brother! I did not wonder that my mother was so troubled.

A few days after this I had to go out with Ginger in the carriage. She did her work honestly, and did her full share, and I never wish to have a better partner in double harness. After we had

been out two or three times together we grew quite friendly and sociable, which made me feel very much at home.

As for Merrylegs, he and I soon became great friends; he was such a cheerful, plucky, good-tempered little fellow, that he was a favourite with everyone.

One night I was suddenly woken up by the stable bell ringing very loud. I heard the door of John's house open, and his feet running up to the Hall. He was back again in no time; he unlocked the stable door, and came in, calling out, 'Wake up, Beauty! You must go well now, if ever you did.'

There was before us a long road and John said to me, 'Now, Beauty, do your best,' and so I did; for two miles I galloped as fast I could. The air was frosty, the moon was bright; it was very pleasant. We came through a village, then through a dark wood, then uphill, then downhill, till after an eight miles' run, we came to the town, through

the streets and into the market-place. The church clock struck three as we drew up at Dr White's door. John rang the bell twice, and then knocked at the door like thunder. A window was thrown up, and the doctor, in his night-cap, put his head out and said, 'What do you want?'

'Mrs Gordon is very ill, sir; master wants you to go at once; he thinks she will die if you cannot get there. Here is a note.'

'Wait,' he said, 'I will come.'

He shut the window and was soon at the door. 'The worst of it is,' he said, 'that my horse has been out all day, and is quite done up; my son has just been sent for, and he has taken the other. What is to be done? Can I have your horse?'

'He has come at a gallop nearly all the way, sir, and I was to give him a rest here but I think my master would not be against it, if you think fit, sir.'

'All right,' he said, 'I will soon be ready.'

The doctor was a heavier man than John, and not so good a rider; however, I did my very best. Soon we were in the park. My master was at the Hall door, for he had heard us coming. He spoke not a word; the doctor went into the house with him, and Joe led me to the stable. Joe Green, the stable boy, tried to take care of me. He was young and small, and as yet he knew very little, but I am sure he did the very best he knew. But soon I began to shake and tremble, and turned deadly cold; my legs ached, my loins ached, and my chest ached, and I felt sore all over. I could not draw my breath without pain.

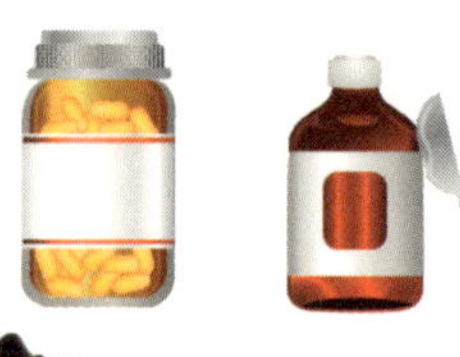

John nursed me night and day. My master, too, often came to see me.

'My poor Beauty,' he said one day, 'my good horse, you saved your mistress' life, Beauty; yes, you saved her life.'

I was very glad to hear that, for it seems the doctor had said if we had been a little longer it would have been too late. John told my master he never saw a horse go so fast in his life.

I had lived in this happy place three years, but sad changes were about to come over us. Our master and mistress had to leave the house for a warmer climate as the mistress was very ill.

Master sold Ginger and me to an old friend. Merrylegs he had given to the vicar, but it was on the condition that he should never be sold, and that when he was past work he should be shot and buried. John went on to be a horse trainer.

The next morning John put the saddle on Ginger and the leading rein on me, and rode us across the country to Earlshall Park to live with an earl. We were taken to a light airy stable, and placed in boxes adjoining each other, where we were rubbed down and fed. In about half an hour John and York, who was to be our new coachman, came in to see us.

John said, 'I don't believe there is a better pair of horses in the country. The black one is the most perfect temper I ever knew. But the chestnut, I fancy, must have had bad treatment.'

'Of course,' said York, 'I quite understand. I'll do my best to take care of them, but that's all I can do.'

They were going out of the stable, when John stopped, and said, 'I had better mention that we have never used the check-rein with either of them; the black horse never had one on, and the dealer said it was the gag-bit that spoiled the other's temper.'

'Well,' said York, 'if they come here, they must wear the check-rein. I prefer a loose rein myself, and his lordship is always very right about horses but my lady—that's another thing; she will have style, and if her carriage horses are not reined up tight she wouldn't look at them. I always stand out against the gag-bit, and shall do so, but it must be tight up when my lady rides!'

John came round to each of us to pat and speak to us for the last time; his voice sounded very sad. I held my face close to him; that was all I could do to say good-bye; and then he was gone, and I have never seen him since.

The next day the Earl came to look at us; he seemed pleased with our appearance. York then told him what John had said about us.

'Well,' said he, 'you must keep an eye to the mare, and put the check-rein easy; I dare say they will do very well with a little humouring at first. I'll mention it to your lady.'

In the afternoon we were fastened and put in the carriage and led round to the front of the house. We heard the rustling sound of silk as my lady came down the flight of stone steps. She was a tall proud-looking woman, and did not seem pleased about something, but she said nothing, and got into the carriage. This was the first time of wearing a check-rein, and I must say, though it certainly was a nuisance not to be able to get my head down now and then, it did not pull my head higher than I was trained to carry it. I felt anxious about Ginger, but she seemed to be quiet and content.

The next day the mistress said, 'York, you must put those horses' heads higher, they are not fit to be seen.'

York got down, and said very respectfully, 'I beg your pardon, my lady, but these horses have not been reined up for three years, and my lord said it would be safer to bring them to it by degrees; but, if your ladyship pleases, I can take them up a little more.'

'Do so,' she said.

York came round to our heads and shortened the rein himself, one hole, I think. Every little makes a difference, be it for better or worse, and that day we had a steep hill to go up. I had to pull with my head up now and the strain came on my back and legs. When we came in, Ginger said, 'Now you see what it is like; but this is not bad, and if it does not get much worse than this I shall say nothing about it.'

Day by day, hole by hole, our bearing-reins were shortened, and instead of looking forward with pleasure to having my harness put on, as I used to do, I began to hate it. Ginger too seemed restless, though she said very little. The worst was yet to come.

One day my lady said again, 'Are you never going to get those horses' heads up, York? Raise them at once, and let us have no more of this humouring nonsense.'

York drew my head back and fixed the rein so tight that it was almost intolerable; then he went to Ginger, who was impatiently jerking her head up and down against the bit, as was her way now. She took her opportunity and started kicking and jumping. She fell down and York sat himself down flat on her head to prevent her struggling, at the same time calling out, 'Unbuckle the black horse! Run for the winch and unscrew the carriage pole! Cut the trace here, somebody, if you can't unhitch it!' The groom soon set me free from Ginger and the carriage, and led me to my box. There I stood, angry, sore in my leg, my head still strained up to the saddle, and no way to get it down. I was very

miserable, and felt much inclined to kick the first person who came near me.

Before long, however, Ginger was led in by two grooms, a good deal knocked about and bruised. York came with her and gave us orders, and then came to look at me. In a moment he let down my head.

Ginger was never put into the carriage again, but one of the earl's sons was sure she would make a good hunter. As for me, I was obliged still to go in the carriage, and had a fresh partner called Max; he had always been used to the tight rein. I asked him how it was he bore it.

'Well,' he said, 'I bear it because I must but it is shortening my life, and it will shorten yours too, if you have to stick to it.'

'Do you think,' I said, 'that our masters know how bad it is for us?'

'I can't say,' he said, 'but the dealers and the horse-doctors know it very well. The fashionable people want their horses to carry their heads high and to step high. Of course, it is very bad for the horses, but then it is good for trade. The horses soon wear up, and they come for another pair.'

In my old home I always knew that John and my master were my friends; but here, although in many ways I was well treated, I had no friend.

York might have known, and very likely did know, how that rein troubled me; but I suppose he took it as a matter of course that could not be helped; at any rate, nothing was done to relieve me.

No doubt a horse fair is a very funny place to those who have nothing to lose; at any rate, there is plenty to see.

I was sent to a horse fair to be sold. The gentlemen always turned from me when they saw my bad knees, though the seller who had me swore it was only a slip in the stall.

There was one man, I thought, if he would buy me, I should be happy. He was not a gentleman. He was rather a small man, but well made, and quick in all his motions. I knew in a moment, by the way he handled me, that he was used to horses; he spoke gently, and his grey eye had a kindly, cheery look in it.

'Well, old chap,' he said, 'I think we should suit each other. I'll give twenty-four for him.'

'Say twenty-five, and you shall have him.'

'Twenty-four ten,' said my friend, in a very decided tone, 'and not another sixpence—yes, or no?'

'Done,' said the salesman; 'and you may depend upon it there's a cruel deal of quality in that horse, and if you want him for cab work he's a bargain.'

The money was paid on the spot, and my new master took my halter, and led me into a very narrow street, with rather poor-looking houses on one side, and what seemed to be coach-houses and stables on the other.

I was put into a comfortable, clean-smelling stall with plenty of dry straw, and after supper, I lay down, thinking I was going to be happy.

My new master's name was Jeremiah Barker, but as every one called him Jerry, I shall do the same. Polly, his wife, was just as good a match as

a man could have. She was a plump, trim, tidy little woman, with smooth, dark hair, dark eyes and a merry little mouth. The boy, named Harry, was nearly twelve years old, a tall, frank, good-tempered lad and little Dorothy (Dolly they called her) was her mother over again, at eight years old. I never knew such a happy, merry family before or since.

The next morning, when I was well-groomed, Polly and Dolly came into the yard to see me and make friends. It was a great treat to be hugged again and talked to in a gentle voice, and I let them see as well as I could that I wished to be friendly. Polly thought I was very handsome, and a great deal too good for a cab, if it was not for the broken knees.

'Of course there's no one to tell us whose fault that was,' said Jerry, 'and as long as I don't know I shall give him the benefit of the doubt for a firmer, neater stepper I never rode. We'll call him 'Jack', after the old one—shall we, Polly?'

'Do,' she said, 'for I like to keep a good name going.'

Jerry had a cab of his own, and two horses, which he drove and attended to himself. His other horse was a tall, white, rather large-boned animal, called Captain.

Jerry took as much pains to see if the collar and bridle fitted comfortably as if he had been John Manly over again. There was no check-rein, no curb, nothing but a plain ring snaffle. What a blessing that was!

The first week of my life as a cab horse was very trying. I had never been used to London, and the noise, the hurry, the crowds of horses, carts, and carriages, that I had to make my way through, made me feel anxious and disturbed but I soon found that I could perfectly trust my driver, and then I made myself easy, and got used to it.

Jerry was as good a driver; and what was better, he took as much thought for his horses as he did for himself. In a short time I and my master understood each other, as much as a horse and a man can do. In the stable, too, he did all that he could for our comfort. He kept us very clean, and gave us as much change of food as he could, and always plenty of it; and not only that, but he always gave us plenty of clean fresh water.

One day, while our cab and many others were waiting outside one of the parks where music was playing, a shabby old cab drove up beside ours. The horse was an old worn-out chestnut, with an ill-kept coat, and bones that showed plainly through it, the knees bend over, and the forelegs were very unsteady. There was a hopeless look in the dull eye that I could not help noticing, and then, as I was thinking where I had seen that horse before, she looked full at me and said, 'Black Beauty, is that you?'

It was Ginger! But how she changed! The beautifully arched and glossy neck was now straight, and lank, and fallen in; the clean, straight legs and delicate fetlocks were swelled; the joints were grown out of shape with hard work; the face, that was once so full of spirit and life, was now full of suffering, and I could tell by the heaving of her sides, and her frequent cough, how bad her breath was. She had been sold many times since we last met.

I said, 'You used to stand up for yourself if you were ill-used.'

'Ah!' she said, 'I did once, but it's no use; men are strongest, and if they are cruel and have no feeling, there is nothing that we can do but just bear it. I wish I was dead. I have seen dead horses, and I am sure they do not suffer pain.'

I put my nose up to hers, but I could say nothing to comfort her. I think she was pleased to see me, for she said, 'You are the only friend I ever had.'

Just then her driver came up, and with a tug at her mouth, backed her out of the line and drove off, leaving me very sad, indeed.

A short time after this, a cart with a dead horse in it passed our cab stand. The head hung out of the cart tail, the lifeless tongue was slowly dropping with blood; and the sunken eyes! It was a chestnut horse with a long, thin neck. I saw a white streak down the forehead. I believe it was Ginger; I hoped it was, for then her troubles would be over. Oh! If men were more merciful they would shoot us before we came to such misery.

Many years passed. From a colt I had grown into a horse. I had been sold to and owned by various men during those years, some of whom were cruel. It was at a sale that the kind groom Mr Thoroughgood and his grandson Willie eventually bought me. I was happy in my current home.

On a summer day the groom cleaned and dressed me with such fantastic care that I thought some new change must be at hand; he trimmed my fetlocks

and legs, passed the tarbrush over my hoofs, and even parted my forelock. I think the harness had an extra polish. Willie seemed half-anxious, half-merry, as he got into the chaise with his grandfather.

'If the ladies take to him,' said the old gentleman, 'they'll be suited and he'll be suited. We can but try.'

Three ladies came out of the house I was taken to and looked at me and asked questions. The younger lady—Miss Ellen—took to me very much.

The next day, when my groom was cleaning my face, he said, 'That is just like the star that Black Beauty had, he is much the same height, too; I wonder where he is now.'

He began to look me over carefully, talking to himself.

'White star in the forehead, one white foot on the off side, this little knot just in that place'; then, looking at the middle of my back—'and as I am alive, there is that little patch of white hair that John used to call 'Beauty's threepenny bit.' It must

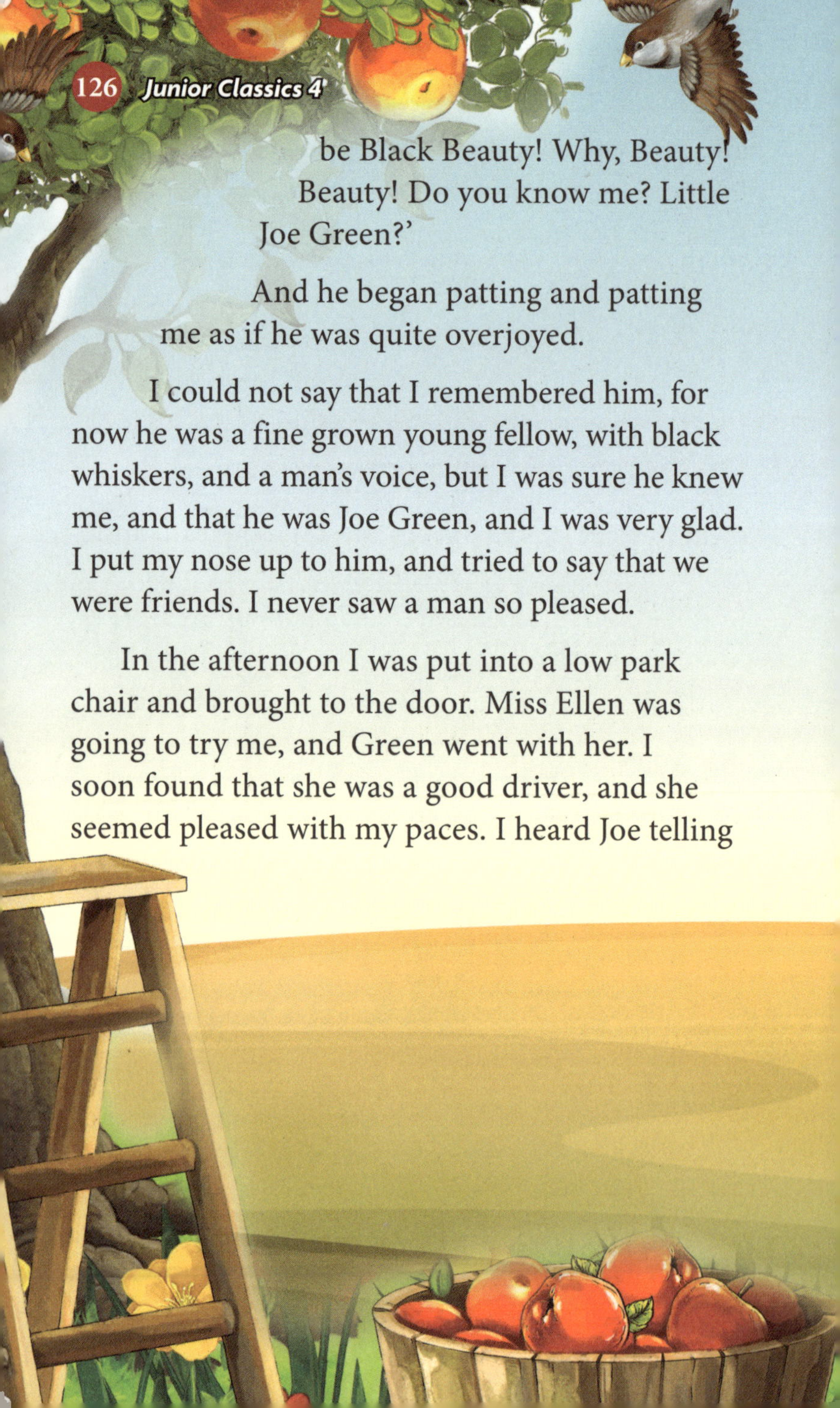

be Black Beauty! Why, Beauty! Beauty! Do you know me? Little Joe Green?'

And he began patting and patting me as if he was quite overjoyed.

I could not say that I remembered him, for now he was a fine grown young fellow, with black whiskers, and a man's voice, but I was sure he knew me, and that he was Joe Green, and I was very glad. I put my nose up to him, and tried to say that we were friends. I never saw a man so pleased.

In the afternoon I was put into a low park chair and brought to the door. Miss Ellen was going to try me, and Green went with her. I soon found that she was a good driver, and she seemed pleased with my paces. I heard Joe telling her about me, and that he was sure I was Squire Gordon's old 'Black Beauty.'

I have now lived in this happy place a whole year. Joe is the best and kindest of grooms. My work is easy and pleasant, and I feel my strength and spirits all coming back again. Mr Thoroughgood said to Joe the other day: 'In your place he will last till he is twenty years old—perhaps more.'

Willie always speaks to me when he can, and treats me as his special friend. My ladies have promised that I shall never be sold, and so I have nothing to fear; and here my story ends. My troubles are all over, and I am at home; and often before I am quite awake, I fancy I am still in the orchard at Birtwick, standing with my old friends under the apple trees.

Other Titles *In the* Series

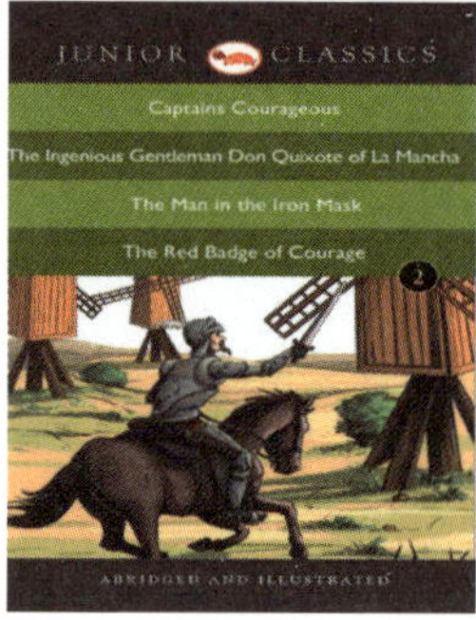

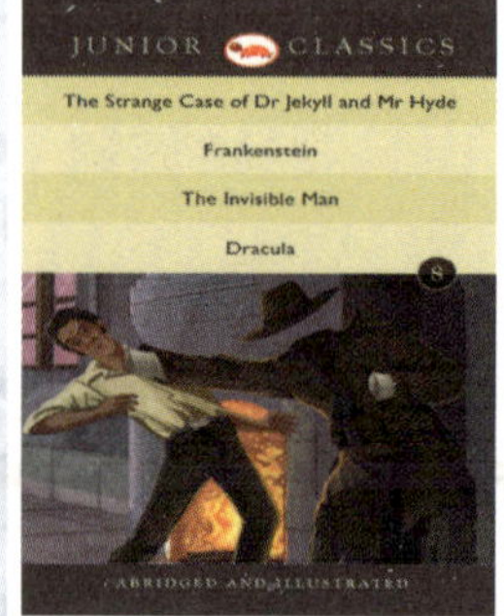

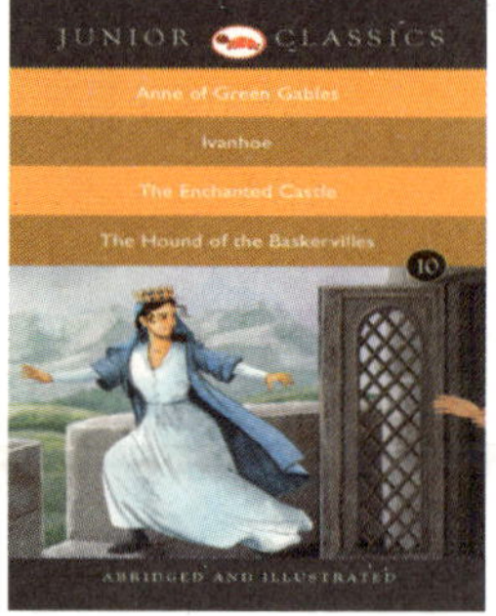